T0167091

BOOKS BY JAY R. LEACH

How Should We Then Live
Behold the Man
The Blood Runs Through It
Drawn Away
Give Me Jesus
A Lamp unto My Feet
Grace that Saves
The Narrow Way
Radical Restoration in the Church
Manifestation of the True Children of God
According to Pattern
Battle Cry
Is there not a Cause?
We Would See Jesus
According to Pattern 2nd ED.

ACCORDING TO PATTERN

Understanding the Deeper Truths of God

SECOND EDITION

JAY R. LEACH

Order this book online at www.trafford.com
or email orders@trafford.com

Most Trafford titles are also available at major online book retailers.

Print information available on the last page.

ISBN: 978-1-4907-9972-8 (sc)
ISBN: 978-1-4907-9971-1 (e)

Library of Congress Control Number: 2020902657

Trafford rev. 02/07/2020

www.trafford.com

North America & international
toll-free: 1 888 232 4444 (USA & Canada)
fax: 812 355 4082

THIS BOOK IS DEDICATED TO MY WIFE MAGDALENE, A TRUE AND DEVOTED HELPMEET – WHO HAS SO OFTEN BEHIND THE SCENES HELD UP MY DROOPING ARMS – WITH DEEPEST GRATITUDE.

CONTENTS

SECTION V   FARTHER ALONG

SECTION VI   GET THE REAL THING

SECTION VII I BELONG TO HIM

SECTION VIII STANDING ON THE PROMISES

SECTION IX   CONTEND FOR THE FAITH

INTRODUCTION

Are you spiritually following God's biblically
revealed truth, "According to pattern?"

This book is not written to merely provide information. It is meant to change your life. It invites you to a deeper relationship with God the Father, Jesus Christ, and the Holy Spirit through a journey into the unknown. The heart of the message found in this book – will renew your mind through the revealed knowledge of the deeper truths of God and transform all your relationships.

Some time ago I heard two preachers' comments concerning the tabernacle of Moses, each on a different Christian television show on the same day. One said, "The tabernacle is of no use today because it is Old Testament." The second preacher spoke of the importance of the *study* of the tabernacle as God's *pattern* through which the believer is enabled to see and understand the absolute deeper truths of God's amazing grace and mercy. His *eternal pattern* of salvation for a lost world – through the perfect sacrifice, our Lord and Savior, Jesus Christ is unchangeable. I agree with the second preacher.

Their discussions give rise to the question: "Is the study of the tabernacle important for believers today?" Yes! Undoubtedly the tabernacle was important to God, He devoted two chapters in the Bible to the Creation, as compared to more than forty chapters throughout the Old and New Testaments covering the tabernacle [the study reveals the true New Testament believer-priest/ mature disciple's walk in the Spirit and his or her *understanding* of the deeper truths of God].

This book grew out of my deep concern over ever-increasing challenges to the "deeper biblical truth of God's Word" and the Christian's lack of spiritual growth to mature disciples in our local churches. All due to the believer's inability to understand and receive a certain body of Truth, which is of things *"revealed" unto us [only] by the Spirit."* Emphasis added. The tremendous importance and accuracy in unveiling the earthly *pattern* of the true tabernacle in heaven itself; comes into full focus as the Spirit of truth *reveals* these important "truths," I will list a few examples that He reveals:

- The deeper things of God for a spiritually mature life of power and blessing
- How to be a living sacrifice
- How to get your prayers answered
- How to get to heaven
- How to enter God's presence
- Who can enter God's presence?
- Spiritual and moral absolute "truths" required to get there
- Absolute proof of only "one Way" to God

The "pattern" of God's great grace, provision and mercy is clearly revealed throughout; coupled with His assurance of spiritual growth and blessings for those who love Him. Through obedience and application of His Word as led by the Spirit of truth – we search out the revealed biblical truths typified in every aspect of the tabernacle. The deep truth found herein is what the great theologian Francis Schaffer often referred to as "true truth!"

In the movie "The Ten Commandments," a traditional monumental hit during the passion-week each year, Charlton Heston in the role of Moses descended Mt. Sinai carrying the two tablets containing the Ten Commandments [*the Law*] written by the finger of God. We are very familiar with that scene though it is Hollywood's entertainment version.

The Scriptural truths of the event are preached and taught in our Sunday school lessons, Bible studies and Bible stories. But few people are familiar with the instructions God also gave Moses on that same occasion "in the Mount"(see Exodus 24:18), concerning the detailed construction of the tabernacle, a house of God. It was God's desire to dwell among His people.

Every detail of construction had to be "according to pattern." Obedience to God's pattern was required of those persons involved. The Spirit came upon *all* those involved in any and all aspects of the construction, operations and functions of the tabernacle (see Exodus 31:1-7). The Spirit of God came upon a select few in pre-cross days. However, in contrast, He is available for all New Testament believer-priests.

Absolutely nothing was left to human imagination – nor is anything left to be modified or upgraded by any individual or church today concerning God's pattern for salvation (see John 3:16), and the required consecrated, holy and transformed life (see 1 John 3:16). Neither is the provision and protection that is to follow salvation to be tampered with. We are to be guided *only* by the Holy Spirit and the truth of God's Word, which always work together for good. Sadly, much of what is believed about God, Christ and the Holy Spirit today is 2nd or 3rd hand. In fact, for the greater part of local churches today, it's mere hear-say information? This is due mainly to failure to fulfill Jesus' Great Commission, *"Teaching them to obey."* Therefore, syncretism, aberrant doctrine, and blatant heresy remain in the churches around America and the world. We must restore authentic Christian theological education and training. All disciples can and must be in the knowledge of the truth for themselves!

A brief survey of the tabernacle reveals the *non-negotiable* absolute biblical and spiritual truths *revealed* by the Spirit for the New Testament believer-priests. God's redemptive pattern of salvation and reconciliation remains unchanged throughout the ages.

God's entire plan and operation thereof was provided through His mercy, [not giving us what we do deserve] and grace, [unmerited favor] offered in the death, burial, and resurrection of His Son, Jesus Christ to a totally lost world. There is no other way!

True believer-priests are those who embrace these absolute truths of Christ's *finished* work on the Cross by grace through unwavering faith, in Him! This book is written on the established biblical truth that:

1. There is absolute spiritual and biblical moral truth in the world today established by God's Word and revealed to the children of God by the Holy Spirit.
2. In spite of the efforts of postmodern and post Christian thought such as moral relativism, political correctness, the new tolerance, multiculturalism, and other man-made "isms" with their many variations – God's truth is absolute, immutable and eternal.
3. The tabernacle was constructed to provide a house for God that He could dwell among His people, the Scripture records, "It was the pattern of things to come."

Even today in the twenty-first century, we gain much understanding from a prayerful study of that pattern. However, these truths can be realized *only* by those who are "born again from above" (study John 3:3 and Romans 1:9-10).

- God's love and redemption [through the blood of Jesus]
- God's dwelling is us [true believers only]
- Christ in the tabernacle [we are the temple]
- God's standards of holiness [live "as unto the Lord"]
- How to come to heaven [pure in heart]
- How to approach the throne of grace [not without sacrifice]
- How to get a prayer through [with no unconfessed sin]
- The absolute truth about sin in the believer's life after salvation [abide in Christ who is Truth]

In studying the typology of the tabernacle, I have observed some important focal points that will clarify, enable, and strengthen the walk of any true believer-priest who adheres to them through personal spiritual and biblical obedience in application ["according to God's pattern"].

I have listed a few, but in no way is the list complete or in any specific order or preference:

- New Testament believers must be "born again" "born from above" (see John 3:3-8).
- We are a new creation (II Corinthians 5:17).
- We have been reconciled to God through Christ and He has given to us the ministry of reconciliation (see II Corinthians 5:18).
- We have the righteousness of God and His Son Jesus Christ (see II Corinthians 5:21).
- We have a personal relationship and fellowship with God and Christ through the Holy Spirit (1 John 1:3).
- Believers are to obey God rather than man (Acts 5:29).
- The necessity of purity in the believer's presenting his or her body a living sacrifice unto the Lord (see Romans 12:1, 2).
- The answered prayers of the righteous (see Psalm 66:18).
- The true believer clearly understands that the only way to God and His heaven is through His Son, Jesus Christ (see Matthew 6:33).
- The true believer walks through grace by faith not by sight (II Corinthians 5:7).

- The absence of Satan and the world in the believer's salvation – as salvation is of God (Acts 4:12).
- The believer's utmost dependence is upon the Lord for everything (see James 4:10).
- Jesus Christ is Lord (see Mark 2:28).
- The "finished work" of Jesus Christ is our only way to God (John 14:6).
- Jesus Christ is our only way to heaven (John 14:6).
- Jesus Christ is our only hope of glory (Romans 5:2).
- The tabernacle in the Old Testament typifies Christ, our Sacrifice [once for all] for the sins of the whole world. The pattern through Jesus Christ's finished work demonstrates the same faith, dedication, and walk in the Spirit and the Word of God according to "pattern" under His grace and mercy today. Holiness in tabernacle times [Old Testament] carries the same meaning over into the [New Testament].

In both Testaments the words are used of *things* and of *persons.* When used of things *no moral* quality is implied as is true of people – they are sanctified or *made holy* because they are set apart for God.

I pray that this book will serve as a clarion call to young and old believers alike, who are vying to speak with a spiritual voice of revealed biblical truth into this generation; that they may see the world the way Christ sees it and:

1. Revive, reorient and reeducate the local churches to the commands of Christ as found in the Great Commandment (Matthew 22:37-40) and the Great Commission (Matthew 28: 19-20).
2. Bring the church back to its original calling of holiness, power, and fervent prayer! Rather than condemnation, all true believers should be reminded that as New Testament believer-priests we are to daily live out the truths of God's Word before the world. It has been said, "One picture is worth a thousand words."
3. Restore true New Testament believer-priests to become active intercessors and priests to help build-up and fortify the body of Christ. Thus, enabling them through the Spirit and the truthful knowledge of the Word of God to be the "pattern" for Christ

to the world. It is imperative that we stand true to Christ as we interact with people, experience and endure present day temptations and persecutions from an ever-increasing secular culture and ungodly society.

4. Love God and others, win the lost, and live godly lives before the world, encourage the downtrodden, comfort the hurting, provide spiritual and biblical direction to the weak and backslidden.

5. Save others with fear, pull and snatch them out of the fire through the *resurrection power* of the gospel, clearly sharing the "finished work" of [Jesus Christ] with them (see Acts 1:8; Jude 3).

6. Hating even the garments spotted by the flesh (see Jude 20-25).

I agree with Paul, "… that we may present everyone perfect, [spiritually mature] in Christ Jesus" (see Colossians 1:28). I pray that God will grant us the Spirit of truth, obedience and humility to do this work by faith through His grace, so that all may experience:

"No eye has seen, no ear has heard, no mind has conceived, what God has prepared for those who love Him – but God has revealed it to us by His Spirit" (I Corinthians 2:9-10 NIV).

– Jay R. Leach
Fayetteville, North Carolina

I can say with the Prophet Amos,
"I was no prophet, but a shepherd. And the Lord took me as I followed the flock, and the Lord said unto me, Go prophesy to My people"
(Amos 7:14-15).

SECTION I

According to Pattern!

CHAPTER ONE

God's Commands Are Clear

"For God so loved the world that He gave His only begotten Son that whosoever believe on Him should not perish, but have everlasting life"
(John 3:16)

In the military each level of command has access to a big thick book called the Uniformed Code of Military Justice. Its purpose is to aid the commander in justly meting out appropriate punishment consummate with the infraction committed; to get it wrong could mean legal suicide. It was comprehensive and it seems that all known infractions of law were included in it. Therefore, any imaginable wrong committed is recorded there with the appropriate punishment options.

How much more important it is for us to live in the love of God and the truth of His Word, the Bible; searching the Scriptures daily rather than just make occasional visits there; and become familiar at all with the absolute deeper truths of God. God showed that the sacrifice of His beloved Son on the cross was motivated by His deep love for sinners. Woe, to individual Christians, churches and ministries that compromise God's absolutes [Spiritual laws] with politicians and other influential groups through fear, and possible loss of some secular-based government incentive or entitlement because it is so-called politically incorrect to do so.

Though incorrect these compromises reflect prevalent assumptions in our society. Until these assumptions are shown to be false, our religious freedom will remain threatened. The lack of Spiritual and biblical knowledge is no excuse today – biblical truth is available!

True believers have access to God's deeper revealed truths. Like the Lord commanded Joshua, "this Book of the Law shall not depart from your mouth, but you shall meditate on it in the day and night that you may observe to do according to all that is within it. For then you will make your way prosperous, and then you will have good success"

(Joshua 1:8). God laid these standards on Joshua, who was the busiest man in the entire nation at that time! How are we doing? Are we too busy?

The parts of Scripture that Joshua possessed [Genesis – Deuteronomy], the Torah or Pentateuch, has always been the main spiritual food of those who serve the Lord. The principles found therein are central to all spiritual effort and enterprise, namely the deeper understanding and application of Scripture at all times. We have the same promises and assurance of God's presence and blessing as He promised Joshua. The assurance of God's presence has always been the staying power for all of His true believers at all times. Carefully study,

- Abraham (see Genesis 15:1)
- Moses and his people (see Exodus 14:13)
- Isaiah (see Isaiah 31:10)
- Jeremiah (see Jeremiah 1:7, 8), and
- Believers through the centuries (see Matthew 28:20; Hebrews 13:5)

God does not have to say something more than once for it to be true and important; His extra emphasis on the tabernacle marks it to be vital for us as well. Hebrews 9:24 says the *"holy places"* of the tabernacle were figures of *"Heaven itself."* Figure 1 below depicts the tabernacle:

Figure 1

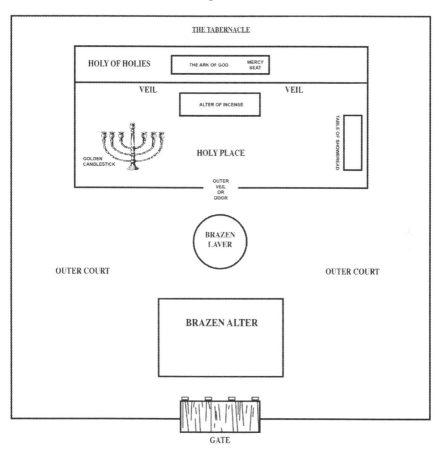

THE TABERNACLE

HOLY OF HOLIES — THE ARK OF GOD — MERCY SEAT

VEIL — VEIL

ALTER OF INCENSE

HOLY PLACE

GOLDEN CANDLESTICK

TABLE OF SHOWBREAD

OUTER VEIL OR DOOR

BRAZEN LAVER

OUTER COURT — OUTER COURT

BRAZEN ALTER

GATE

Christ's sacrifice was superior to the man-made sacrifices under the Mosaic covenant because Christ did not enter a man-made sanctuary, which was a copy, instead, He entered the true sanctuary – which is heaven itself and into the very presence of God.

This being true, the way the priest approached the holy place in the tabernacle is also the way for us to come to heaven. Another motivation for studying the tabernacle in conjunction with your spiritual journey is the fact that the New Testament cannot be fully understood apart from the *truths* depicted therein. **Figure 1** depicts the tabernacle, *the dwelling place* of God:

The tabernacle was surrounded by 75 feet wide by 150 feet long fence with a gate or door facing east. This outer court as it was called depicts the true New Testament believer's earthly walk [life] in relation to God.

Just within the gate, loomed a large **brass altar** where the animals were sacrificed and completely consumed [*corresponding with Christ's sacrificial death on the Cross*]. This practice went on according to pattern for 1500 years. Each sacrifice typified Christ, as He was offered *once and for all* – for the sins of the whole world. All believers should follow Paul's example of love, commitment and dedication to God for His "Unspeakable Gift:"

"For to me to live is Christ, and to die is gain" (Philippians 1:21).

"That I may know him, and the power of his resurrection, and the fellowship of his suffering, being made conformable unto his death" (Philippians 3:10).

When we say "yes" to Jesus Christ, we are redeemed, bought by His blood!

Next in line in the outer court was a **brass laver**, filled with water for the priests to wash their hands and feet before entering the holy place to minister. The laver depicts the New Testament believer-priest confessing his or her sins and being *cleansed* from daily defilement. There are many sins that can haunt and entangle a believer. We must continually be on guard, washing regularly and faithfully by coming to Christ, the Perfect Sacrifice, who alone can wash and cleanse us from sin (see 1 John 1:9).

The importance of the washing was very pointed: the priests must wash or die (v. 21). God is holy and He will not allow any person to bring sin into His presence. The priests' lives depended upon obedience. They could not afford to skip the laver and go straight into the *holy place*; nor could they afford to wait and wash later. God was serious; *"lest you die"* a person had to be cleansed before approaching Him and before serving Him (see Psalm 66:18).

Every believer in every generation, in every culture must be washed and cleansed from the defilement of sin before approaching God. God will cleanse us; this is His promise if we will only cry out for cleansing:

"Wash yourselves, make yourselves clean; put away the evil of your doings from before My eyes cease to do evil" (see Isaiah 1:16; also see 52:11; Psalm 26:6; Acts 22:16).

"In Him we have redemption through His blood, the forgiveness of sins, according to the riches of His grace" (Ephesians 1:7b; also see 2 Corinthians 7:1).

"Therefore, if anyone cleanses himself from the latter, he will be a vessel for honor, sanctified, and useful for the Master, prepared for every good work" (2 Timothy 2:21; also see James 4:8).

"If we confess our sins, he is faithful and just to forgive us our sins, and to cleanse us from all unrighteousness" (1 John 1:9).

"But if we walk in the light, as He is in the light, we have fellowship with one another, and the blood of Jesus Christ his Son cleanses us from all sin" (1 John 1:7).

Once cleansed the priest could enter the tabernacle, *the place of worship.* A rather small building, fifteen feet wide, forty-five feet long, fifteen feet high and covered with unattractive badger skins – but it was exquisite inside. Its door made of the same material as the fence gate parallels *Christ as the door.*

The building was divided into two rooms: the first room was called the *holy place* (see Figure 1). The New Testament believer's position *in Christ* in heaven is depicted in this room.

A holy New Testament priesthood

In I Peter 2:5 the Scripture says, Christians are:
"...... a holy priesthood to offer up spiritual sacrifices acceptable to God. through Jesus Christ.

The Old Testament priest and the New Testament believer-priest share a number of characteristics:

The OT Priests

- Priesthood is an elect privilege (see Exodus 28:1; John 15:16).
- Priests are cleansed of sins (see Leviticus 8:6-36; Titus 2:14).
- Priests are clothed for service (see 2 Peter 5:5; Exodus 28:42; Leviticus 8:7; Psalm 132:9, 16).

- Priests are anointed for service (see Leviticus 8:12, 30; 1 John 2:20, 27).
- Priests are prepared for service (see Leviticus 8:33; 9:4, Galatians 1:16; 1 Timothy 3:6).
- Priests are ordained to obedience (see 1 Peter 2:4; Leviticus 10:1).
- Priests are to walk with God (see Malachi 2:6; Galatians 5:16, 25).
- Priests are to impact sinners (see 2:6; Galatians 6:1).
- Priests are messengers of God (see Malachi 2:7; Matthew 28:19-20).
- Priests are privileged to have access to God – to offer spiritual sacrifices.

The NT believer-priest's Spiritual sacrifices (2 Peter 2:5)

The sacrifices this holy priesthood offers are spiritual:

1. they are holy sacrifices themselves (Romans 12:1-2; 1 Corinthians 2:15; 3:1; Galatians 6:1)
2. services (1 Corinthians 2:4; 9:11; 14:12; 2 Corinthians 3:6)
3. songs (Ephesians 5:19; Colossians 3:16)
4. praises (v. 9; Hebrews 13:15-16)
5. conduct (Romans 8:1-13; Galatians 5:16)
6. personal faith (2 Corinthians 4:15)
7. wisdom and knowledge (Colossians 1:9)
8. personal love (Colossians 1:8)
9. faithfulness (Philippians 1:27; Romans 1:9)
10. prayer and supplications (Ephesians 6:18)

It was the *place of daily fellowship* and *worship* of the priest with the Lord. There were three pieces of furniture in this room through which the priest accomplished his service:

- On the north side stood the table of showbread – the priest's *food*.
- On the south side stood the lampstand for *light*.
- Next to the veil [60 feet tall] that divided the two rooms stood the altar of incense which depicts the *prayers* of the priest ascending as a sweet smell to God. This parallels the prayers of the New Testament believer-priests. [see **Figure 1**]

A very thick and beautiful veil or curtain closed off the last room. This veil represented the flesh or body of Christ which hid the glory of God from outward view and was *torn in two from top to bottom and thrown open at the death of Christ.*

Prior to the death of Christ this cube-shaped final room was called the Holy of Holies, or Holiest of all, into which was placed the Ark of the Covenant. The Ark of the Covenant contained the Ten Commandments on stone, Aaron's rod that budded, and a pot of manna, as memorials. Above the Ark, between the two cherubim, was *where God said He would meet with the high priest,* Aaron. It typifies heaven itself, the dwelling place of God. Exodus 26:18 through the end of the book gives details and descriptions for making the tabernacle and its ministry, "all according to *God's* pattern." All of this is in accordance with God's plan. We should also remember man had no plan of his own! All of life is in the plan of God, who created us. The song writer said, "We can't even walk without Him holding our hand."

As I stated earlier, Moses received two directives from God on Mount Sinai: the Torah and the Tabernacle – Law and Grace. Someone has said,

- The Law showed why no person by him or herself could come to God.
- The Tabernacle showed the way in which a person can come to God.
- On Mount Sinai God pictured the way to heaven.
- On Mount Calvary Jesus Christ purchased the way to heaven.

Spectacular or sensational

Many do not believe that the things of the believers in Christ should be spectacular and therefore to them it is only a spectacle [many in the local church today quickly exclaim, "It doesn't take all of that!"] A simple view of Mount Sinai as Moses received the Law; and on Mount Calvary when our Savior died should open the eyes of all, that God is awesome and spectacular! When the Law was given,

> *"....... There were thunders and lightening, and a thick cloud upon the mount, and the voice of the trumpet exceeding loud; so that all the people that was in the camp trembled. And Moses brought forth the people out of the camp to meet with God; and they stood at the nether part of the mount. And Mount Sinai was altogether on*

smoke, because the Lord descended upon it in fire; and the smoke thereof ascended as the smoke of a furnace, and the whole mount quaked greatly. And when the voice of the trumpet sounded long and became louder and louder, Moses spoke, and God answered him by a voice" (see Exodus 19:16-19).

One of the all-time strategies of warfare has been "shock and awe!" Needless to say both were present on Mount Calvary when the Savior died,

"…. there was darkness over the whole land …. And, behold, the veil in the temple was rent in twain from the top to the bottom; and the earth did quake, and the rocks were rent; and the graves were opened; and many bodies of the saints which slept arose, and came out of the graves after the resurrection, and went into the holy city, and appeared unto many" (see Matthew 27:45-53 KJV).

We are not told what was accomplished by all of this in either case, but it would certainly be an understatement to even hint or simply say it was sensational. Moses was alone with God. To be alone with God would transform any life. Notice Jacob's encounter alone with God, he wrestled with Him until He blessed Him. What a tragedy that we spend so little time with God. No wonder we see so little of His power and glory in our lives and churches today! Such a spiritless relationship reflects a spiritual and biblical ignorance that is invading and negatively affecting the church, along with all other institutions especially traditional marriage and the family, homes, secular public schools, and governments at all levels today.

Back to the Tabernacle

The old radio series, the Lone Ranger use to begin, "Return with us now to the days of yester-year." We preachers and teachers need to return to the holy place of fellowship and worship with the Lord, to feast on the Bread of Life and receive a message from Him for His people, and deliver that message with all of our heart through the power of the Holy Spirit who resides in us!

The purpose of the tabernacle is defined in Exodus 25:8, "and let them make Me a sanctuary; that I may *dwell among them."* It was to be a "sanctuary," a "place set apart" for God to dwell among them. For the first time, God was to have a house of worship. There had been altars such as Abraham's, but no structure had been *set apart for the worship of God*. God had walked with Adam in the Garden of Eden, and had visited with Abraham, and in the tabernacle, He would dwell with Israel. Notice His progression:

- In 2 Chronicles 7:16 we see Him dwelling in the temple.
- In Colossians 2:9 we see Him in His Son.
- In 1 Corinthians 6:9-20 we see Him in the believer.

The tabernacle had to be portable, because the children of Israel had not come into their new homeland yet. They were pilgrims in a foreign land. Today we also are pilgrims and have a portable place of worship:

"For you are the temple of the living God; as God has said, I will dwell in them, and walk in them; and I will be their God, and they shall be my people" (2 Corinthians 6:16).

Like Israel, we also are not home yet! We are "strangers and pilgrims" in a foreign land (see 1 Peter 2:11). Many believers would never consider desecrating their church building:

- Yet, many Christians carelessly involve themselves in sinful practices that are harmful to their body, which is the temple of the Holy Ghost, and never give it a second thought.
- We "set apart" the church building for the worship of God and certainly we ought to respect it. But when we leave the church building, we do not leave the glory of God there as did the Israelites in the tabernacle.
- We should ever be conscious of Christ in us wherever we go (see Colossians 1:27). *"That I may dwell in them."*

He did not come to dwell among them because they were holy – but to make them holy. God's pattern in the tabernacle shows the New Testament believer-priest the way to God. It tells on what basis a person can meet with God and commune with Him, and how God and the believer can dwell together here and, in the hereafter, (see Revelation 21:3). Again, nothing is left to human thoughts or modifications. God's Word is true and every man a liar! Truth matters!

According to pattern

In Hebrews 9:23-24 we are told, *"It was necessary that the patterns of things in the heavens should be purified with these; but the heavenly things themselves with better sacrifices than these. For Christ is not entered into the holy places made with hands, which are the figures of the true; but into heaven itself, now to appear in the presence of God for us."*

So *only* "according to pattern" we can come into God's presence by "the heavenly things themselves with a better sacrifice," *even Christ's precious blood* **[this is God's pattern throughout the ages]**. The high priest went every year alone into the holiest of all – into God's presence, which is a picture of heaven itself, but *"not without blood"* (see Hebrew 9:24).

The one absolute essential that we must have to stand before God is not our church membership, baptism or our works. We absolutely cannot stand before God without the blood of Jesus Christ!

We must come before God "not without blood," for "without shedding of blood is no remission" (Hebrews 9:22).When the sinner brought his lamb for a sacrifice to the priests at the brazen altar he had to lay his hands on the head of the animal to identify [himself and his family] with it. The brazen altar typifies the cross and Christ, the sacrifice for our sin. We must identify with Him on the cross. When we were God's enemies, Christ was able by His death to reconcile us to God. Certainly, now that we are children of God, the Savior can keep us by His mighty resurrection power (see Romans 5:10).

This teaching must be made clear to those seeking salvation. By faith, be sure you apply the **blood** of Jesus to your own heart and life so that God can see it as the atonement **for your sins**. Christ suffered and died on the **cross for your life**, and you can stand before God completely washed from all sin, a new creation, if you claim Christ and His sacrifice for yourself. He died that we might live! A divine exchange took place; Christ took my sins and **gave me His righteousness:**

"For He has made Him to be sin for us,
who knew no sin.
that we might be made

the righteousness
of God in Him."
– (II Corinthians 5:21)

And now I am a new creation in Christ, all things are made new:

"Therefore, if any man be in Christ,
he is a new creature:
old things are passed away;
behold all things are become new."
– (II Corinthians 5:17)

The holy place

As stated earlier, the holy place typified the New Testament believer's daily fellowship with God in worship, the Word, and prayer. The Old Testament tabernacle was according to God's pattern, and parallels not only our salvation but also our holy Christian living. God was present in the Holy of Holies of the tabernacle; thus, He met with His people.

Although there is no tabernacle today – Jesus Christ is within all true believers to produce fruit through them. Just as there was only one way to approach God in the tabernacle, so there is only one way for believer-priests to produce fruitful lives (see Romans 5:9-10). **That one way** was specified by the Lord Jesus Christ Himself. He told all true believers to,

"Abide in Me, and I in you." As the branch cannot bear fruit of itself, except it abide in the vine; no more can you, except you abide in Me. I am the vine, you are the branches: he that abides in Me, and I in him, the same brings forth much fruit: "for without Me you can do nothing" (John 15:4, 5). Emphasis added.

The only way the believer-priest's life can be pleasing to God is for him or her to abide in fellowship with Him. The Christian out of fellowship produces no fruit!

Patterns and parallels

The entire tabernacle: the building, furniture, and priestly ministry – was a type of perfect Christ. *All had to be according to what God revealed.* Thus, any deviation from God's pattern in the tabernacle would bring death. Even though we are not under the law system today, anyone who tries to come to God by any way other than Jesus Christ faces spiritual blindness and death. There is *no other way* of salvation (see Acts 4:12).

Therefore, the remainder of this book's focus will mainly be the operation and significance of each piece of furniture in the tabernacle and how its revealed truth parallels the salvation, present walk, and fruitful life of all true New Testament believer-priests. All are in type of the priest's entrance into the holy place; and the believer's entrance into heaven and the very presence of God **(see Figure 1 on page 16).**

REFLECTION AND DISCUSSION QUESTIONS: CHAPTER 1

1. How does the way the Old Testament priest's approach the holy place parallel the New Testament believer-priest's approach to the throne of grace today?

2. Discuss how Christ is pictured in the tabernacle?

3. Does God allow sin in His presence? If not why not?

4. How does the operation at the brazen altar parallel the cross and the believer's life today?

5. Discuss how the three pieces of furniture in the holy place parallel the believer's spiritual experience under grace today?

6. I can apply this lesson to my life by:

7. Closing Statement of Commitment:

CHAPTER TWO

The Bread of Life

*"For Christ has not entered the holy places made with
hands, which are copies of the true, but into heaven itself,
now to appear in the presence of God for us"*
(Hebrews 9:24).

The social privileges of New Testament believer-priests are not presented in the Old Testament or in the gospels; they are revealed in the New Testament Epistles. There were five inspired writers of the Epistles: Paul, Peter, James, John and Jude. In Galatians 2:9, Paul referred to Peter, James, John and Jude as "pillars." All five of these men were pillars of the church in that they *upheld* Christ's foundational teachings concerning what was necessary for fellowship with Him.

The door to the holy place was set in a foundation of brass (see Exodus 26:37). Brass symbolizes judgment, in this case, the judgment of Christ for sin. These pillars pointed toward the complete judgment of Christ, and as such upheld the entrance [curtains] made possible by the finished work of Christ [Calvary].

So, these curtains of entrance reminded the worshipper that Christ is the door because of His suffering and death on behalf of humanity. Jesus referenced the purpose of the curtain when He said, "I am the way, the truth, and the life: no man [or woman] comes to the Father, but by Me" (see John 14:6). Emphasis added throughout.

Seven Pieces of Furniture

The tabernacle contained seven pieces of furniture. Seven is the number of perfection [God's complete provision] in the Bible for those who are *in Christ*.

We have already considered the altar and the laver located in the outer court in detail. It bears repeating, the altar was a picture of the cross of Christ. He purchased our redemption through the shedding of His blood. Remember, "Without shedding of blood is no remission" (Hebrews 9:22). In the cross the New Testament believer-priest receives new life (a new creation) in the death, burial and resurrection of Jesus Christ (study carefully Romans 4-8:1).

The laver also located in the outer court [see **Figure 1**] next to the tabernacle, was for washing of the priest's hands and feet. Thus, it speaks of *separation from the world and cleansing from defilement.* The laver reminds us of the Word of God – because we are *"clean through the Word"* (John 15:3). In his book, *The Saving Life of Christ,* Major W. Ian Thomas offers the following concerning our being in Christ, "To be in Christ is redemption; but for Christ to be in you – that is sanctification! To be in Christ, makes you fit for heaven; but for Christ to be in you – makes you fit for earth! To be in Christ, changes your destination: but for Christ to be in you changes your destiny! The one makes heaven your home – the other makes this world His workshop.[1]

Once the priest stepped inside of the Holy Place, he was in **the place of fellowship.** On the right was the table of showbread, on the left was the golden candlestick and straight ahead was the altar of incense **(see Figure #1 on page 16).** We will cover each of the three pieces separately in some detail. Though each was a separate piece of furniture, each related to the others. In fact, it is impossible to understand the full significance of one without understanding the others. (Emphasis is mine throughout).

The Table of Showbread (Exodus 25:23-24)

The purpose of the showbread was to provide food for the priests as they ministered in the tabernacle worship and service (see Leviticus 24:9). This eating was done as an act of worship and spiritual fellowship with the Lord.

The table of showbread speaks of Christ, the Living Word through the written Word, Bread of life, on whom we are to feed to receive our spiritual nourishment for growth and maturity. The more we behold *"the glory of the Lord"* in the Word of God *"with open [unveiled] face,"* we are *"changed into the same image from glory to glory, even as by the Spirit"* (2 Corinthians 3:18). We can learn some very important lessons by seeing:

- The place in which it was eaten was "the holy place" (see Lev. 24:9).
- The holy place was the first room inside the darkened tabernacle. It is the place of fellowship with the Lord.

- It meant the priest had been to the brazen altar – which typified the cross of Christ and the saved believer-priests.
- The priest had washed in the laver *"lest he die,"* which meant confessing sin and cleansing from daily defilement since they left the brazen altar, parallels the New Testament believer-priest confessing his or her daily sins and being in perfect fellowship with the Lord. Now, inside the holy place with no unconfessed sin – they can have fellowship and communion with the Lord and partake of spiritual food.
- These truths perhaps explain why so many of God's children do not feed on the Word of God. They are out of fellowship with the Lord; just as would be a priest outside the tabernacle – needing their feet and hands cleansed from defilement. *"If I regard iniquity in my heart, He will not hear me"* (Psalm 66:18).
- Sin in the life of a believer-priest ruins his or her spiritual appetite for God's Word.

Sin will keep you from the Word – or the Word will keep you from sin.

The reason some people get so much from the Word and have *fresh truths* to teach others is that they are in fellowship with the Lord and spend time in His presence feeding on His Word (see 2 Timothy 2:2). As we study God's Word, we must look for the Lord Jesus, who is the Bread of Life on every page and, as we see Him and become more like Him.

The table of showbread was only about two feet high, making it accessible only to a bending or kneeling person. The Word of God is accessible only to a person who *humbles* them self before a holy God. Today those believer-priests who humble themselves before the Lord and spend time in His presence are illuminated to receive *revealed* truths in the Word of God that even those with great intellect cannot see without the Holy Spirit. We see higher on our knees in His presence at the table of the Lord than any other place.

The Golden Lampstand (Exodus 25:20-21)

The lampstand on the other side of the Holy Place shined its light on the table of showbread which typifies [the deeper things of God] and the altar of incense typifies the [prayers of the righteous] and the cherubim on the veil to the Holy of Holies, representing guardians of the holiness of God. It was to provide its light continually in the presence of the LORD, both day and night. The light in the Holy Place represented Jesus Christ in all His purity. This is a vivid reminder to us of what the Bible says concerning Christ:

> *"This then is the message which we have heard of Him, and declare unto you, that God is light, and in Him is no darkness at all. **If we say that we have fellowship with Him and walk in darkness, <u>we lie</u>**, and do not practice the truth. But if we walk in the light as He is in the light, we have fellowship with one another, and the blood of Jesus Christ His Son **cleanses us from all sin"*** (1 John 1:5-7). Emphasis added throughout.

The holy place was completely sealed preventing *any* light what-so-ever from the outside entering into the holy place. In the tabernacle, the light parallels God through Christ by the Holy Spirit, shining in the darkness, thus producing a place of fellowship and communion. Anything that needed to be confessed would be *revealed* in the place of fellowship as the light shined on the table of showbread and the altar of incense. And as was true then is also true today:

> *"But if we walk in the light, as He is in the light, we have fellowship one with another, and the blood of Jesus Christ His Son cleans us from all sin"* (1John 1:7).

The light of the Word of God is the only true light and safe guide. And the intercessory prayer life is effective only as it is fulfilled in the true light of the Holy Spirit.

Jesus said of Himself as the Light of the World: *"As long as I am in the world, I am the light of the world"* (John 9:5). Then Jesus said to them, *"A little while longer the light is with you, walk while you have the light, lest darkness overtake you; he who walks in darkness does not know where he is going. While you have the light, believe in the light, that you may become "sons of light"* (John 12:35-36).

Thus, the lampstand was the vessel that illuminated the priest's view. The tent would have been a dark, unknown mystery. Likewise, without the illumination of the Holy Spirit in the human heart we would:

- Be stumbling about in darkness
- Be fearful

- Be foolish
- Be confused
- Be helpless
- Be hopeless
- Be subject to false teaching
- Be subject to false worship
- Be lonely
- Be empty

The lampstand illuminated *the way into God's presence and showed the priests how to walk into His presence.* [Paralleling the New Testament believer-priest's walk in the Spirit] Note the instructions:

- A command was given to provide pure olive oil to keep the light burning continually (v. 20). The lamp of God was to give brilliant, bright, pure light. The source of the light was from the pure olive oil.
- The command was a permanent law – to be kept by all generations (v. 21). This is significant – God's light, is for all generations, for every man, woman, and child throughout the ages.

Barna research has revealed that only 25% of Christians in America believe in the very existence of the Holy Spirit and His work – what does that mean for the other 75%? Also, there are 2 billion Christians of varying degrees worldwide, which means there are 5 billion people without Christ in the world:

- When the light of God [the Holy Spirit] is hidden from people – the darkness brings destruction and death.
- When the light of God is shielded from the acts of sinful people – their hearts become hardened.
- When the light of God is extinguished – people follow false gods.
- The light of God must be kept burning or else the world will be lost in darkness.

In 2 Timothy 3, Paul prophesied that these very characteristics would mark the end time worship; when people would have a form of godliness but deny the power [the Holy Spirit] there of.

Throughout Scripture oil symbolizes the Holy Spirit. We must be filled with the Holy Spirit so the world can see Christ and His great love for them through us *continually.* Every believer-priest is challenged to have a life marked by the fullness of the Holy Spirit. The Spirit-filled believer bears a strong witness of love, joy, and peace:

> *"And do not be drunk with wine, in which is dissipation; but be filled with the Spirit ......"* (Ephesians 5:18).

> *"But the fruit of the Spirit is love, joy, peace, longsuffering, gentleness, goodness, faith, meekness, temperance, against such there is no law"* (Galatians 5:23).

There is some controversy in the church concerning Spiritual gifts (see 1 Corinthians 12) and the fruit of the Spirit. Many churches set a great priority on receiving the gifts but place little or no attention on the cultivation of the fruit of the Spirit (see Galatians 5:22-23).

However, like the Holy Spirit and the Word of God; the fruit and gifts of the Spirit work in tandem. Any other offers result many times in people who because of [pride] or some other sinful reason allowing their gifts to outrun their fruit. Once in the limelight many fall into temptation, selfishness and other unfruitful sins of the flesh, which does much damage to the body of Christ.

There are different kinds of spiritual gifts, but all are resident in the Holy Spirit. If you will open yourself to God's Spirit and submit your spirit fully to Him, through His leading you will find the place where you are meant to serve using the gift(s) given. Study carefully the spiritual gifts listed in 1 Corinthians 12 and the operation of the gifts in chapter 14 but realize that no gift can be activated without the *unconditional* love *("agape" Greek)* of chapter 13 within us.

In whatever place of service you are called to minister in your [Spiritual gift (s)] and serve, your ultimate purpose is to bring glory and honor to God by knowing Him, being like Him, abiding in His will, in His Word, and His ways. He develops the fruit in us through our new divine nature. The fruit are characteristic of Christ and is God's original intention for His children. The fruit analogy is reminiscent of Jesus' teaching on the vine, branches and fruitful harvest (see John 15:1-5).

As we study the Word of God, we are enabled by the Holy Spirit to understand the deeper things of God. We then grow in grace and the knowledge of our Lord and Savior, Jesus Christ – the Bread of Life. As part of Christ's body, you and I have a specific destiny to fulfill as we participate in His mission to reconcile the world by loving God with all our being and loving our neighbors as ourselves. Oh! What a fellowship – what a joy divine, leaning on the Everlasting Arm.

Again, the lampstand provided the only light within the tabernacle (see Exodus 25:37). Only the light which God specified was allowed in the building. Only the Holy Spirit can illuminate the hearts of people.

A REMINDER: The world's knowledge has absolutely no light to throw on the Word of God or the Person of Christ!

Only the Holy Spirit can illuminate truth concerning the Word and Person of Christ in our heart. The lampstand like the rest of the furniture and everything else in the tabernacle; was made according to pattern (see Exodus 31:1-11). We are not left to our own imagination or ideas concerning our living a godly life, just as the Jews in the construction and operation of the tabernacle. God has already given the expectations of the New Testament believer-priests "It is written" according to *His* pattern only!

The Altar of Incense (Exodus 30:34-38)

We now turn our attention to the altar of incense. This altar was positioned next to the veil that provided entrance to the Holy of Holies. No doubt every priest that came into the holy place to offer incense was aware that just beyond the veil was the Mercy Seat where God dwelt with His people **(again see Figure 1)**. Concerning the altar, God told Moses, "You shall make an altar to burn incense on ………..." (see Exodus 30:6).

The altar of incense was to be overlaid with gold and a gold molding (v. 3) the other pieces of furniture in the tabernacle like the Altar of incense was also covered with gold. The most precious metal of all was God's preference for construction of this Altar of intercession.

Remember, gold is a symbol of deity, The golden altar is a symbol of our most prized possession the Lord Jesus Christ......God Himself, who is the Perfect Intercessor, the One who lives forever to make intercession – to passionately pray for the children of God.

> *"Therefore, He is also able to save them to the uttermost that come to God through Him, since He always lives to make intercession for them"* (Hebrews 7:25).

Christ can save us because He is fully God and fully man (see 2:18; 4:15). Since this verse speaks of Jesus' present intercession for us, the word "save" in this verse speaks of our *sanctification,* the continuing process by which we are freed from the power of sin.

This continuing process of salvation will eventually be completed in our *glorification when we are saved from the presence of sin.* Therefore, the word indicates that Jesus continues to save those who keep coming to Him. Our *justification* is a once-for-all event accomplished through Christ's finished work; however, our *sanctification* is an ongoing process.

Our prayers should always be fervent, and as hot as the coals on the altar. Prayer is not a time for complacency but for the deep cry of the human spirit to touch the living God!

> *"The righteous cry out,*
> *and the Lord hears,*
> *and delivers them out of all troubles.*
> *The Lord is near to those who have a broken heart,*
> *and saves*
> *such as have a contrite spirit."*
> – (Psalm 34:17, 18)

> *O God, You are My God;*
> *Early will I seek You;*
> *My soul thirsts for You;*
> *My flesh longs for You*
> *In a dry and thirsty land*
> *Where there is no water.*
> – (Psalm 63:1)

The altar of incense was to be the place where permanent incense ascended to the LORD (Exodus 30:8). This symbolized two commands:

1. There is the symbol of the permanent intercession of Jesus Christ. He died and arose from the dead for this very purpose: to stand before God as the Great Intercessor for us.
2. There is the symbol that believers are to pray morning and evening, to pray always, to develop an unbroken communion with God, to never cease being in a spirit of prayer.

"Seek the LORD and His strength, seek His face continually" (1 Chronicles 16:11).

"Ask, and it will be given to you; seek, and you will find; knock and it will be opened to you" (Matthew 7:7).

"Praying always with all prayer and supplication in the Spirit, being watchful to this end with all perseverance and supplication for all saints" (Ephesians 6:18).

God's people are to pray wherever they go, anyplace, anywhere, and anytime. The inner veil that had once separated the altar of incense from the Ark of God's presence was thrown open, ripped from top to bottom by God Himself through the death of His Son, the Lord Jesus Christ. The way into God's presence is now open. We are now invited to come boldly and worship God at the throne of grace.

> *"Let us therefore*
> *Come boldly*
> *To*
> *The throne of grace,*
> *That we may*
> *Obtain mercy, and*
> *Find grace*
> *To*
> *Help in time of need."*
> – (Hebrews 4:16)

We should especially take note how forcefully God stressed the holiness of the altar of incense:

- The priests were never to allow the altar to be desecrated nor misused (Exodus 30:9).

  Any foreign thing that was placed on the altar was a direct affront to God. Prayer is holy to God. It is more intimate than any physical relationship experienced by people. Adding anything to God's plan was and is sin.

- For the altar of incense to have any lasting significance, it had to be directly connected to the blood that was shed on the altar of burnt offerings. Why? Because the prayers of believers must be directly connected to the shed blood of Jesus Christ (v. 10).

It is at the altar of prayer where we plead the power of Christ's blood to cleanse us.

It is at the altar of prayer where we stand in Christ reconciled to God.

It is at the altar of prayer in Christ's name where we come into and experience the wonderful presence of God Himself.

In His presence

We are to come boldly to the throne of grace, directly into God's presence and look on the Mercy Seat. As we come to God in prayer, we need to realize that we come to the throne of grace and whatever we receive is because of God's mercy:

- We deserve nothing.
- We should have a deep sense of our undeserving worthiness before God.
- There are those who come before God demanding or some even commanding things of God, which indicates that they are not conscious of looking on the Mercy Seat.
- Although we are "heirs of God and joint-heirs with Christ" (Romans 8:17) – in the flesh we are conscious of our unworthiness before a holy God.
- God said, "If my people, which are called by my name, shall humble themselves, and pray, and seek my face, and turn from their wicked ways: then I will hear heaven – and heal the land" (2 Chronicles 7:14).
- "God resists the proud but gives grace unto the humble" (James 4:6).

Intercessors for the saints

Christ is our Advocate[2] and Intercessor[3] our prayer must go through Him to the Father. He is our Intercessor who, *"ever lives to make intercession for us"* (Hebrews 7:25) at the right hand of the Father. The Apostle John also emphasized Christ's intercessory ministry for believers:

"My little children, these things I write unto you, that you do not sin. And if any man sin, we have an advocate with the Father, Jesus Christ the righteous" (1 John 2:1).

The Apostle asks, "Who is he that condemns?" "It is Christ that died, yes rather, that is risen again, who is even at the right hand of God, who also makes intercession for us" (Romans 8:34).

1. Whereas the **brazen altar** located just inside the curtain fence in the outer court, speaks of the cross and Christ, who died for us.
2. The golden **altar of incense** located in the holy place near the veil, speaks to us of Christ, who lives in heaven to intercede for us.
3. **Redemption** and **reconciliation** took place at the brazen altar.

Intercession for the redeemed took place at the golden altar of incense. Thus, the altar of incense speaks of our living, resurrected, ascended Lord and Savior, Jesus Christ.

Concerning the death, burial and resurrection of Jesus Christ, the Apostle Paul said,

> *"For I delivered unto you first of all that that which I also received, how that Christ died for our sins according to the Scriptures, and that He was buried and that He rose the third day according to the Scriptures"* (1 Corinthians 15:3, 4).

Think about it! Christ died for us that He might give us every spiritual blessing. That's what Paul meant by:

> *"For if, when we were enemies,*
> *we were reconciled to God*
> *by the death of His Son,*
> *much more, being reconciled,*
> *we shall be saved by His life"* (Romans 5:10).

The Lord Jesus Christ saves us from more than the condemnation of sin. He saves us from everything that contaminates our daily life.

Power in prayer

There is power in prayer directed to God through Christ. If we have the *"faith as a grain of mustard seed"* (Matthew 17:20), we can say to a mountain, *"Be thou removed"* (Mark 11:23) and it will. James says,

"Is any among you afflicted? Let him pray" (5:13). He tells us further that *"that the prayer of faith shall save the sick and the Lord shall raise him up" (v. 15).*

God has also made provision for the believer in prayer today in the Person of the Holy Spirit, who gives light, instructions, and illumination in spiritual things. "In the same way the Spirit also helps our weakness; for we do not know how to pray as we should, but the Spirit Himself intercedes for us with groaning too deep for words" (Romans 8:26, NASB).

- He shows us how to pray.
- He helps us to know what to pray for.
- He Himself makes intercession.

Down through the years multitudes of God's children have testified that in times of great distress, when they neither knew how to pray nor what to pray for, somehow it seemed as though, just by groaning from their hearts, the burden of their hearts ascended to God. They sensed in their spirit that God heard their *unvoiced prayer.*

There is real comfort in experiencing this help from the Holy Spirit. Ephesians 8:18 admonishes, "Praying always with all prayer and supplication in the Spirit." Prayer is to be:

- In the light shed by the Holy Spirit.
- In His power and strength.
- Always directed and assisted by Him.

This is the divine provision for prayer to teach us how to pray, and also to know what we should pray.

The Mercy Seat

God tells about the Mercy Seat in Exodus 25:17-22. A slab of pure gold, the same length and width as the ark; and was the Ark's cover (**See Figure 1, page 16).** Made from the same piece of Gold and fashioned at the ends of the Mercy Seat were the cherubim and above the Mercy Seat was where God would meet and commune with Israel.

The Mercy Seat is the place of *union* and *communion* with God. Man can only meet God on His terms at the *blood-sprinkled* Mercy Seat.

When the sinner comes by faith to the throne of grace and claims Christ's blood to satisfy for his or her sins, that person will immediately be born again.

This brings the person into eternal union with God. No longer is he or she seen as in Adam, for now he or she is in the second Adam, Christ and no longer:

- "Without God in the world" (see Ephesians 2:12).
- That person's body becomes "the temple of the Holy Spirit" (see 1 Corinthians 6:19).
- Now that the veil has been torn asunder, we have "boldness to enter into the holiest by the blood of Jesus, by a new and living way, which He has consecrated for us, through the veil, that is to say, His flesh" (see Hebrews 10:19-20).

The word for Mercy Seat is the same word translated "propitiation," which means to appease, or make satisfaction. The work of Jesus Christ is seen as the fulfillment of the Mercy Seat:

"My little children, these things I write to you, so that you may not sin. And if anyone sins, we have an Advocate with the Father, Jesus Christ the righteous. And He Himself is the propitiation for our sins, and not for ours only but also for the whole world" (1 John 2:1-2).

After one is saved, he or she must continually acknowledge and confess sin (see 1John 1:9). However, this does not mean they are powerless against sin. It must be understood by all, fulfilling the duty of confession does not give license to sin. Sin can and should be conquered through the power of the Holy Spirit (carefully study Romans 6:12-14; 8:12, 13; 1 Corinthians 15:34).

Satan accuses believers day and night before the Father due to sin (see Revelation 12:10), however take heart, Christ's High Priestly ministry guarantees not only compassion, but also acquittal (see Hebrews 4:14-16). The sacrifice of Jesus on the cross satisfied the demands of God's holiness for the punishment of the sins for the whole world (see John 1:29; 3:16; 6:51; 1Timothy 2:6; Hebrews 2:9). God is not mad with you, because of His Son's sacrifice in your stead!

REFLECTION AND DISCUSSION QUESTIONS: CHAPTER 2

1. Discuss the table of showbread as it parallels with the deeper things of God in the believer's life today?

2. How do the curtains of entrance in the tabernacle parallel the suffering and death of Christ?

3. Is fellowship with God and Christ mandatory? If so why? What does no fellowship mean to the believer?

4. Discuss what happens in a human heart without the activity of the Holy Spirit?

5. Discuss the significance of the teaching concerning the altar of incense and the Ark of the Covenant in the New Testament believer's life?

6. I can apply this lesson to my life by:

7. Closing Statement of Commitment:

SECTION II

Getting Through to God

CHAPTER THREE

The Right of Access

"Now when these things had been thus prepared, the priests always went into the first part of the tabernacle, performing the services. But unto the second part the high priest went alone once a year, not without blood, which he offered for himself and for the people's sins committed in ignorance; the Holy Spirit indicating this, that the way unto the Holiest of All was not yet made manifest while the first tabernacle was still standing. It was symbolic for the present time in which both gifts and sacrifices are offered which cannot make him who performed the service perfect ...."
(Hebrews 9:6-9). Emphasis added throughout.

The lampstand in the holy place shone not only on the table of showbread and the altar of incense, but it also revealed the cherubim on the veil [curtain] to the Holy of Holies. The cherubim guarded God's holiness – no one was permitted to enter except the high priest once a year.

Jesus was crucified, buried, and rose again to enter the Holy Place into God's presence; so the Light now dwells with God.

Jesus' death tore the veil separating the holy place and the Holy of Holies from top to bottom and made it possible for all believers to enter the presence of God.

"Having therefore, brethren, boldness to enter into the holiest by the blood of Jesus, by a new and living way, which He has consecrated for us, through the veil, that is to say, His flesh; and having an High Priest, over the house of God; let us draw near with a true heart in full assurance of faith, having our hearts sprinkled from an evil conscience, and our bodies washed with pure water"
(Hebrews 19:19-22).

Thus, we have the message of how God dwelt with the separation caused by sin to bring man back to His original purpose through Jesus Christ.

"For there is one God, and there is one Mediator between God and man, the Man, Christ Jesus" (1 Timothy 2:5).

God made man for His own pleasure, that He might enjoy fellowship with His creatures. What hope could there be of man ever approaching the throne of God's holiness without the presence and work of the Mediator Christ Jesus? Jesus Himself said, *"No one comes to the Father, but by Me"* (John 14:6).

The Torn Veil [Curtain]

Christ's death, burial, resurrection, and ascension have torn the curtain apart and opened the way for man into the otherwise *inaccessible* presence of God. The Apostle Peter puts it this way:
"For Christ also died for sins once for all, the righteous for the unrighteous, that He might bring us to God" (1 Peter 3:18).

Church history reveals that this work of Christ as mediator is a truth that became hidden in the medieval period but was brought fully into the light during the Reformation – and is dear to the hearts of all true believers. We have no need of a human priest or intermediary, for we have one great High Priest in the presence of God for us.

Through Christ every true believer has the right of direct access to God. It is good to be reminded that we can never approach God, whether in prayer, praise, supplication or intercession – except through Christ.

Right of access

Even though we have the right of access through Christ, many believers still have problems getting through to God in prayer. It's like the adage, which goes something like, "I know God heard prayers in the past and He hears prayers today, but He won't hear me!" Certainly, we see unbelief here. True hearing begins with a right relationship with God, which is the pattern seen in the tabernacle, the right of access means the right to draw near with boldness. Knowing this – still too many:

- Their prayer life is lacking in fulfilment.
- God is far away from them.

The simple explanation in most cases may be a matter that has been prevalent throughout – even though we have the right to come to the throne of grace; *we are still required to come with clean hands and a pure heart into God's presence.* Some people insist on coming to God on their own terms! God forbid!

Only after confession of known sin and the honest renunciation of it is the death of Christ and the power of His blood available for us to draw near to God.

- Nurturing sin in our hearts stops God's ear (see Isaiah 59:2; Psalm 66:18).
- Disobedience of any kind puts up impenetrable barriers to our prayers and keeps us distanced from God.

God's remedy for sin

If we are conscious of "something" but don't have any idea what it is that's breaking our fellowship and keeping us out of touch with the Lord. We do know that to be restored to God's fellowship, we must:

- Seek the Lord, for the Holy Spirit is waiting to reveal it.
- Humble ourselves before God in confession, renunciation and if necessary, restitution.

The Scripture says, *"If we confess our sins, He is faithful and just to forgive us our sins and to cleanse us from all unrighteousness"* (1 John 1:9).

This powerful passage includes *all* believers who confess [acknowledge] sin. God says that we are sinners in need of forgiveness. To confess is to agree with God, to admit that we are sinners in need of His mercy. Forgiveness and cleansing are guaranteed because God is faithful to His promises. On the other hand, the Scripture continues,

"If we say that we have not sinned, we make Him a liar, and His Word is not in us" (v.10).

To make this denial is clearly calling God a liar because God's Word says, "We all have sinned, and come short of the glory of God" (Romans 3:23).

Remission is essential

The psalmist said, "If I regard iniquity in my heart, He will not hear me" (Psalm 66:18). Many people today even some in the church seem to act prideful over the fact that they can carry a grudge or unforgiveness in their hearts, all due to spiritual and biblical ignorance. The Greek word translated "remission" in Matthew 26:28; Acts 10:43; Hebrews 9:22 rendered "forgiveness." *It means to send off, or away.* And this, throughout Scripture, is the fundamental meaning of forgiveness. Distinction must be made between *divine* and *human* forgiveness:

- Human forgiveness means the remission of penalty.
- In the Old and New Testament, in type and fulfillment, the divine forgiveness follows the *execution* of the penalty.

"The priest shall make an atonement for his sin that he had committed, and it shall be forgiven him" (Leviticus 4:35 KJV).

"This is my blood of the new testament, which is shed for many for the remission of sins" (Matthew 26:28 KJV).

"Without shedding of blood there is no remission" (Hebrews 9:22 KJV).

- The sin of the justified believer interrupts his or her fellowship with the Lord and is forgiven upon confession, but always on the ground of Christ's propitiating sacrifice (see 1 John 1:6-9; 2:2 KJV).
- Human forgiveness rests upon and results from the divine forgiveness. In many passages of Scripture this is assumed rather than stated, but the principle is declared in (Ephesians 4:32; Matthew 18:32, 33).

The first mention of sacrifice is Genesis 3:21, wherein God made the "coats of skins" having obviously come from slain animals for Adam and Eve. The first sacrifice with clarity is Genesis

4:4; which is explained in Hebrews 11:4. When the law was instituted an order of priests was established who alone could offer sacrifices. As stated in our discussion of the tabernacle, those sacrifices were "shadows," types expressing the guilt and need of the offerer in reference to God – and all of them pointed to Christ as they were all fulfilled in Him.

Understanding the above Scriptures, denying that sin is in us *indicates* that God's Word is not in us. In other words, the Word *is not* changing their life.

Did we miss something?

I pray that we did not miss the major point God made in the Old Testament and particularly the tabernacle. There God made it clear that He would not put up with our mingling together the unholy with the holy [clean]. Why was there such an emphasis put on a separated priesthood in the Old Testament?

God put much emphasis on a separated priesthood to *give us* an example of His firm commitment to reveal Himself *only* through a holy, [cleansed], and separated people.

A clean people

*For if the blood of bulls and goats and the ashes of a heifer; sprinkling the **unclean,** sanctifies for the purifying of the **flesh** – how much more shall the **blood of Christ,** who through the eternal Spirit offered Himself without spot to God, **cleanse your conscience** from dead works **to serve** the living God?* (Hebrews 9:13-14). Emphasis added throughout.

It seems nothing is more intolerable and ignored today in the churches than a defiled conscience – a conscience polluted by sin and oppressed with guilt. Once it's in the saddle, it refuses to be silenced. Even in the holiest conditions it suggests its message of condemnation, which produces the following:

- Communion with God is immediately cut off.
- Boldness of access into His presence becomes mere memory.

- As the light of God's countenance fades the enemy can secure an easy victory.
- Joy fades away and service quickly becomes drudgery.
- Peace and victory distances themselves closer to non-existence.

The sad part is all of this has happened because the conscience has been defiled. We know that God has made provisions for every other malady and heart need, so we can rest assured that He didn't leave out cleansing of the polluted conscience. The reference to the "red heifer" in Hebrews 9:13-14 carries us back to the tabernacle times of the Old Testament, especially to the strange ceremony recorded in Numbers 19.

This ordinance of the red heifer is surprisingly not found in Leviticus, generally the priest's book of instructions, but in Numbers, the book of Israel's wilderness sojourn. It is worthy to note, that in each of the Pentateuch's books there is a chapter which foreshadows some aspect Christ's death. Additionally, please note the following parallels Old Testament events:

In Genesis 22, Abraham's offering of Isaac we are presented the mysterious picture of the cross:

- The infinite cost to the Father of the sacrifice of the Son.
- The willingness of the Son to obey His Father's will in the divine plan of redemption.

The Passover night recorded in Exodus 12 representative of the blood of the innocent victim applied in faith to stay the execution of judgment on the first born. Again, in Leviticus 16 which details the ritual of the great Day of Atonement. There the death of Christ is representative of both satisfying both the righteous claims of God against sinners and forever bearing away his polluting sins.

In Numbers 19 taken in conjunction with Hebrews 9:13-14, we are presented to the sacrificial death of Christ:

- God's provision for the maintenance of unbroken communion with Him.
- God's permanent provision for the *constant cleaning* of the believer as he or she walks amid inescapable daily life defilement.
- In Christ's atonement, sins of the future are in view as well as sins of the past, and sins of which we are unconscious as well as those we are presently conscious of.

No room for sin

These provisions by no means provide permission to sin. If fact it is in sync entirely with:

- Paul's question and answer, *"Shall we continue in sin?" "God forbid"* (Romans 6:1-2).
- John had this concern for the believers when he clearly expressed:

  "My little children these things write I unto you, that you sin not" (1 John 2:1a).

- *"And if any man sin, we have an advocate with the Father, Jesus Christ the righteous"* (2 John 1b).

  Jesus Christ is the Advocate for sinning saints which He carries on with the Father whereby, because of His eternal sacrifice, He restores them to fellowship (also see Psalm 23:3; John 13:10).

- In the same passage, John recognizes the *possibility* of sinning and *reveals* the remedy for such condition:

  "If we confess our sins, He is faithful and just to forgive our sins and cleanse us from all unrighteousness" (1 John 1:9).

Worldly defilement

The world leaves its defiling marks on our robes daily. It's impossible for us to escape defilement. Conversations, television, movies, media, advertisements of the world each bring their own quota of defilement.

If the home and church are not carefully guarded the undetected contamination of sin can be the unconscious means of allowing the subtle atmosphere of the world to infiltrate and defile.

Defilement of the works in many churches has become the norm, due to assimilation with the works of the flesh, as the result of spiritual and biblical ignorance. Sin in the believer's life in the church is much more serious than the sinner on the outside, because his or her guilt is proportioned to privilege.

Ecclesiastical defilement

The epistle to the Hebrews states that the works of the person whose *conscience is defiled* are only "dead works" and can never satisfy the living God. They are just what the words imply including:

- All service is initiated without the Holy Spirit.
- All services are prompted by self; these works may be right in themselves but are done from unspiritual motives.
- All prayers are heartless.
- All preaching is powerless.
- All services are loveless.

On recent Love Worth Finding broadcast, the late Dr. Adrian Rodgers made the following observation in his sermon concerning the church today. He stated that two thirds of Christians are unsaved. Therefore, he offers the following three groups of people on the church roll:

1. Cultural Christians – they joined the church because they did not want people to think they are atheists.
2. Congregational Christians – don't care about the Bible, God, Christ, the Holy Spirit or the church, it's just a good place to meet people.
3. Convictional Christians – a spiritually robust people of the Word who loves the Lord and divine truth, which they apply to their daily life.

REFLECTION AND DISCUSSION QUESTIONS: CHAPTER 3

1. Discuss the significance of the torn veil in the tabernacle and the doctrine of the priesthood of all believers.

2. How does the right of access affect New Testament believers today?

3. Discuss several reasons many believers will not come boldly to the throne of grace?

4. What affect does sin in your heart have on your prayer life?

5. What is the biblical significance of "clean hands" in reference to a defiled conscious?

6. I can apply this lesson to my life by:

7. Closing Statement of Commitment

CHAPTER FOUR

The Power of Access

"For through Him we both have access by one Spirit to the Father"
(Ephesians 2:18).

Once we have thoroughly examined ourselves before the Lord with without conviction there should be nothing to hinder our getting through to God. In the verse above we see the Spirit has a vital part to play in our getting through. Paul is teaching here that our access to God through Christ is in the power of the Holy Spirit.

In fact, all our fellowship and worship with God is dependent upon the activity of the Holy Spirit. When we hear the benediction pronounced, ending with the words, *"the fellowship of the Holy Spirit be with you all"* (see 2 Corinthians 13:14); and notice it is a fellowship with the Father and with His Son Jesus Christ initiated and maintained by the Holy Spirit.

After I returned from the war in Vietnam and was assigned to Fort Knox, Kentucky I received an order to report to the Headquarters to receive a medal for my actions in combat. The order gave me a right to enter the Commander's presence. It took me pass the guards that would normally stop anyone from entering the Headquarters without proper permission.

But having entered the General's presence – if left to myself in that maze of offices and vast corridors, I would have no doubt gotten lost, arrived late or totally missed the appointment. I needed a guide from the General's staff to conduct me personally into the Commanding General's presence.

I had to submit to the escort's guidance, obey his instructions, and wait to be announced and received. Nothing was left up to me. The order got me into the building, but the guide had to conduct me into the General's presence. We have access, but only by the Holy Spirit.

Coming into the Presence of God

The finished work of Christ has provided us the right of access or entry into God's presence, but the indwelling Spirit is also needed to:

- Instruct and conduct us into God's presence.
- Make access to God a reality.
- Bring to us the deep conviction so that we don't waste words in prayer.
- Enable us to communicate face to face with a loving heavenly Father.
- Provides the answer to our weakness in the matter of getting a prayer through to God.
- The Mercy Seat has also revealed the mercy that God could and would extend to a sinful people – if they came into *His* presence the prescribed way.

Religionized Christianity

Many sermons and lessons presented today lead people to believe that by their performance they can reach up to God and with a certain attitude, rituals and works He will meet their every command or wish. This theology would make Christianity just another religion, which would please many people today. More and more people in this beautiful country are willing to accept this pseudo-religionized Christianity because there is little commitment, responsibility or accountability required on their part as a religion.

The term Christian originally denoted a new way of thinking and a changed life in Christ. However, the definition has become so secularized, broadened, and flexible supposedly so that one size fits all. As a result, many churches are accepting people into membership and totally omitting the necessity of even knowing Christ and His work on the cross. Christians in increasing numbers in some pulpits as well as pews are denying the apostolic doctrines essential for true believers. They deny:

- The deity of Christ.
- The virgin birth of Christ.
- The atonement of Christ.
- The coming judgment of the world by Christ.
- The future kingdom whose King is Jesus Christ.

- The heaven for believers and a future hell for unbelievers.
- The supernatural.

Make-up your own

To the world the gospel is too restrictive and the Bible too intolerant, their displeasure has sent secular thought, moral uncertainty, and doctrinal confusion throughout the American church convincing even some denominations that our commission is no longer valid concerning the "going into all the world" preaching the gospel to every creature, to the saving of souls. It seems that more people are going forth into all the world more concerned about saving animals and the environment than the souls of people. In fact, you are more likely to be considered *un-Christian* today if you don't buy into the pluralism, politically correct mind-sets of the secular humanists, environmentalists, abortionists and gay agenda.

Therefore, to them to call anything sinful is unloving and would mean that you are not a good Christian. Many church members today have convinced themselves that it is their right to sin if it gets what they want. In fact, adultery, cohabitation and illegitimacy are accepted as normal conduct and behavior and can be listed among the "silent issues of many local churches." The issues are there; but never addressed, nor are the people involved called into account. This behavior grieves the Holy Spirit and is a disservice to the churches involved (see 1 Corinthians 5 and 6).

Church discipline

Church discipline is a dinosaur to many in the church because it was put on the shelf decades ago by the carnally minded as no longer needed. Through this unscriptural attitude toward sin, much of the church in America has lost their zeal and therefore compromised their commitment to the deeper truths of God's Word and living righteous lives of love and compassion.

I've heard it from many parents, "let them go and it's up to them what they do about Christ!" "That's their personal choice!" "Hands off no coercing allowed." Over the years many local churches in America have forgotten their God-given mission for edification [building up the body]. Today we have a generation of Christless, Spiritless and biblical illiterate children roaming the aisles of our churches with no knowledge of the true and Living God. Cursing, they attempt to work though the problem [their way] with very little or no concern for others.

In the early church, Paul addressed the problem of church discipline. Notice in 2 Thessalonians 3:14 He instructs the Thessalonians to discipline one of their church members. What is church discipline and when should it be employed? Church discipline is the denying or withdrawal of fellowship to a believer who is involved in open sin, for example:

- Those involved sexual immorality (see Matthew 18:15-17; 1 Corinthians 5:9-13).
- Those creating division within the body of Christ (see Romans 16:17; Titus 3:10).
- Those in open defiance of God's appointed leadership in the church (see 2 Thessalonians 3:6, 7, 14; Hebrews 13:17).

The church must exercise discipline as the church must remain pure (see 1 Corinthians 5:8).

The objective in church discipline is three-fold:

- the repentance of the sinning person (see James 5:19, 20)
- the restoration of an erring brother or sister (see Matthew 18:15; Galatians 6:1)
- the individual feels ashamed enough of the sin to change (see 2 Thessalonians 3:14).

Undoubtedly church discipline was so important to Christ that in Matthew 5:15-19, He gave the clear Scriptural commands Himself on how to handle it:

- If your brother or sister sins against you, go and tell him or her, the fault between the two of you alone. If he or she hears you, you have gained a brother or sister (v. 15). Paraphrase mine.
- If he or she will not hear, take with you one or two more, that *'by the mouth of two or three witnesses every word may be established* (v. 16).
- If he or she refuses to hear them, tell it to the church.

If he or she refuses even to hear the church. The church then is to do everything possible to convince the sinning believer to be reconciled or to right the wrong. If the erring one will not positively respond that person is to be disciplined by being cut off from the fellowship (v. 17).

While expulsion may be painful for the brother or sister; it will actually be better for them and the church – they may repent and return, and the church remains pure. To continue as if the Lord did not mean what He said, the church may find itself as the church in Revelation 3:1-2, God said to that church,

"I know your works; you have a reputation of being alive, but you are dead."

Organism or organization

Many church leaders deny the necessity of the atoning blood of Jesus today. In fact, many don't believe that salvation must involve the cross of Christ at all. We can blame much of this on spiritless, secularly oriented organizational forms, which deny the power of God. I've heard it said repeatedly – even though the church is a "living organism," we have got to have "organization" to deal with the people [members]? It seems that the first order of business is to establish:

- A manageable "discipline" of some sort that expresses in simple language the "dos" and "don't (s)" as a body [*to identify/ look alike/ and act like*].
- Then they establish their own language so we can communicate with one another – with words such as [*born again/ rapture/ trinity*].
- Some even still try to set the length of hair and fashion standards.
- Like the early Scribes and Pharisees, many local churches have gotten so good at rules and laws [doctrines of men] until the "organism" is overshadowed by "organization." Therefore, the term "organism" is heard of only in Bible Colleges and seminaries.
- Much of our preaching turned from the saving gospel of the Kingdom to what "we "do" or "do not do." They are preaching "another gospel," deserving the same rebuke that Paul gave the Galatians.
- Many of our churches have blended into hybrids [a mixed seed, a little of this and a little of that]. Organization came along as a means to an end, but man has made it the end. Chrislam is a good example.

We often hear well-meaning pillars saying, "My church!" We hear this so much until if children pick it up, they translate it to mean "Grandpa's," or "Grandma's," or Reverend "So and So's" church. They never learn whose church it really is many times until they leave home and attend a Bible-believing church – they find out that deacon so and so is not the head of the church. Christ is the Head!

I hope I was not too dramatic here, but it is very crucial that we understand this arrangement belongs strictly to humans – somewhere along the line it stopped being an "organism" to settle for just being *religious*, it's more comfortable! Everything is "cut and dried," "no surprises" and definitely "no changes!" There is no place for God, Christ, the Holy Spirit and the true saints are kept at bay here – therefore they are of little use as the salt and light of the world.

Someone has said, "If you look for the church, you'll find it in the world and if you look for the world it is in the church! I say, "If we aren't careful both will be AWOL!"

The study of the tabernacle shows that to try and reach up to God though any works-performance or *any* other natural means will prove futile. God has come down to us and provided the only and total way [pattern] for sinful humanity to be reconciled to Him. Religion teaches many ways to God. Christ is God's "One and only way!"

True Bible-based Christianity teaches only one-way to God, our Lord and Savior, Jesus Christ – the Author and Finisher of our faith. I repeat in the tabernacle God left nothing to man's imagination nor did He seek human opinions or advice. Simple obedience is the requirement for one coming to God and "not without blood" remains the same today in salvation.

God's mercy revealed

The mercy seat revealed the mercy that God has extended to sinful people, providing they came by His prescribed way. The way was clearly marked: "come by means of a *blood sacrifice*" only! Then the blood had to be sprinkled on the mercy seat in order to satisfy the holy demands of God. Romans 3:23 says,

"All have sinned and come short of the glory of God."

The following Scriptures reveal how God was satisfied concerning man's sin:

"Being justified freely by His grace through the redemption that is in Christ Jesus: whom God has set forth to be a propitiation though faith in His blood, to declare His righteousness for the remission of sins that are past, through His forbearance of God; to declare, I say, at this time His righteousness: that He might be just, and the justifier of him which believes in Jesus" (Romans 3:24-26).

Now the veil is torn and thrown open, God says we can have:

"Boldness to enter into the holiest by the blood of Jesus, by a new and living way, which He has consecrated for us, through the veil, that is to say, His flesh" (Hebrews 10:19-20).

Although an *individual* cannot satisfy for his or her own sins, Jesus Christ died on the cross and became "the propitiation for our sins: and not ours only, but also for the sins of the whole world" (1 John 2:2).

In his wonderful book, *"The Normal Christian Life,"* Watchman Nee, says the blood of Jesus deals with what we have done and the Cross deals with what we are.

The blood disposes of our *sins,* while the Cross strikes at the root of our capacity for *sin.* He uses the analogy of sin being a factory and sins the product produced, so through our being crucified with Christ the factory our old [sin nature] is shut down/ closed/ out of commission].[4]

The story is told of a lady whose husband passed away after a long marriage. She missed him so much that rather than burying him she had his body prepared and preserved sitting in his easy chair encased in glass. She had it positioned in the living room so that she could see him when going out and upon entering the house. After some time, she decided to go on a tour of Europe. While on tour there she met a very nice American widower, they fell in love and got married. After a while they decided to return to the United States.

They decided to live in her very comfortable home. Upon arrival at the home he unlocked the front door. He picked up his bride to carry her across the threshold, she turned on the light and there sat old John in his chair staring at them. Tired she decided to rest awhile. He grabbed the telephone directory flipped through yellow pages until he found a man with backhoe for hire.

He had the man to come over and dig a very, very deep hole into which they placed old John still upright in his stuffed chair and buried him. He exclaimed to his wife, "I'm your new husband now – the old one is dead and buried!" Once we are saved, we receive a new divine nature – we are a new creation (see 2 Corinthians 5:17).

That is how we must treat our old sin nature once we are saved – bury it deep, dead bodies [of sin] lying around can contaminate!

Jay R. Leach

Because Christ fully satisfied the holy demands of God for our sin, God is completely just in extending righteousness to the one who places his or her faith in Christ. It bears repeating! God did not overlook sin; rather, His demands were fully satisfied in the Person of Jesus Christ.

The ark, (see Exodus 25:10-16) signified that God was present among His people. It was the base of His throne, and as such the most sacred instrument in the tabernacle proper. Today much attention is placed on what Jesus Christ did in loving and caring for people while walking the earth as a Man rather than *who* Jesus is. They want to see Jesus as a great humanitarian rather than our Savior. When we really see who Jesus Christ is, we will better understand and appreciate His work. This is why Paul said, *"That I may know Him"* (Philippians 3:10). He was not satisfied in just knowing about Christ – he wanted to know, Him! Do you know Him?

A common meeting Place

God can meet sinful man only on the basis of His perfect righteousness and His perfect grace. To be effective these two must come together. This meeting happens in the Cross of the Lord Jesus Christ. Although the Old Testament offerings provided a temporary covering, God could deal with His people – they pointed to the Cross and the time when Jesus Christ would be the sacrifice to take away sin forever. In this sense, Jesus Christ was our mercy seat – to receive His righteousness and grace we must come through the cross.

We live in an increasingly secular and anti-Christian world and the ensuing confusion in our churches among millennials has many of them choosing to not stay but involve themselves with many faiths or none.

Many also object to the idea that there is only one way of salvation, but there is no other way, and we should rejoice in the Lord that there is even that one way!

Let's pray for our nation, and pastors and churches. Pray for the president and government officials at all levels; also for Christians in other parts of the world who face persecution and open opposition and forget not the evil cloud of indifference and secular humanism that we see increasing against the truth of God's Word in our nation.

Walking – "according to pattern"

"You are to be holy to me because I, the Lord, am holy, and I have set you apart from the nations to be my own" (Leviticus 19:9, 10).

That is a special message of the Old Testament – the story of a unique separated, people who would maintain God's cause on the earth, through a manifestation of His presence – "according to pattern."

In the New Testament the warning is even stronger in condemning the sin of mixing with the standards of the world. God will not manifest His holy presence to those who are *not* of this world "in their *hearts,"* and yielded only to Him. Notice the strong warning Paul offers against having an attachment with the world:

"Do not be yoked together with unbelievers. For what do righteousness and wickedness have in common? Or what fellowship can light have with darkness? What harmony is there between Christ and Belial? What does a believer have in common with an unbeliever? What agreement is there between the temple of God and idols? "We are the temple of the living God. God said: "I will live with them and walk among them, and I will be their God and they will be my people." "Therefore, come out from them and be separate, says the Lord. Touch no unclean thing, and I will receive you." "I will be a Father to you, and you will be my sons and daughters, says the Lord Almighty" (II Corinthians 6:14-18).

A major requirement for walking in the fullness of the Holy Spirit is to no longer mix with the world and its standards. Satan is aware of that. The Bible says, "Satan knows his time is short." It is so amazing that people blame the direct attack on the biblical worldview, values, morals; and the mayhem we are experiencing in our society today on the environment, politicians and anyone or anything except the influencing power of Satan himself. America has been the major depository of Christianity and its teachings for more than two centuries.

Of course, that fact is obscured by the media and the court of public opinion today, mainly through Satan's exploitation and manipulation of the carnal minds in so many Christians today. The Scriptures warn us of his many devices to deceive us – but he banks on the fact that we won't read and study the Bible as we should. His media promotes money-making schemes through gloom and doom rather than to promote love, joy and peace in the Holy Spirit, which is the kingdom of God. Without proper knowledge of the truth, many in the body of Christ are starving and dying a slow death. God wants the world to see the difference between true believers who love Him and the unbelieving world.

Christ's invitation

We live in a world of increasing turmoil and violence, of frustration and disillusionment, however, there is a rest [*relief from this burden*] for the people of God, in spite of conditions and circumstances. In Matthew 11:28-30, notice Jesus' invitation,

> *"Come to Me, all you who labor and are heavy laden, and I will give you rest. Take My yoke upon you and <u>learn from Me</u>, for I am gentle and lowly in heart, and you will find <u>rest</u> for your souls. For My yoke is easy and My burden is light."*

All around we see the constant uneasy movement of people, as never before in the history of the world. Humanity is haunted with fear. Yet *every* true believer- priest has been given a sure promise of rest – a rest which is not always appropriated and enjoyed. The writer of Hebrews admonishes,

> *"Therefore, since a promise remains of entering His rest, let us fear lest any of you seem to have come short of it. For we who have believed do enter that rest, as He said: "So I swore in My wrath, they shall not enter My rest," although the works were finished from the foundation"* (vv. 1, 3).

The tragic ending in unbelief of the generation of Israelites that God brought out of Egypt serves as a warning for every believer today to enter God's rest, which is *still* offered to the faithful:

Since therefore it remains that some must enter it, and those to whom it was first preached did not enter because of disobedience, again He designates a certain day, saying in David, **"Today,"** *after such a long time, as it has been said:* **"Today, if you will hear His voice, do not harden your hearts."** Emphasis added throughout.

For if Joshua had given the rest; then He would not afterward have spoken of another day. There remains therefore a rest for the people of God. For he who has entered His rest has himself also ceased from his works as God did from His.

Let us therefore be diligent to enter that rest, lest anyone fall according to the same example of disobedience. (Hebrews 4:6-11).

The aim of the writer is to illustrate what has been called the "rest of faith" and to warn of the possibility of falling short of it. He pictures a better rest than that into which Joshua led Israel, therefore it must mean complete deliverance of every enemy of our spiritual life. Notice how Zacharias portrays such a life:

That we should be saved from our enemies, and from the hand of all who hate us ...... To grant us that we, being delivered from the hand of our enemies, might serve Him without fear, in holiness and righteousness before Him all the days of our life (Luke 1:71, 74-75).

In an earlier section, I noted that "deliverance" along with "discipline" must be restored to the body of Christ. The truth is Christ's advent and atonement made possible our deliverance from all spiritual enemies for the enjoyment of a life of restful service. Nothing less than this is the rest, that remains for the people of God – and nothing short of it is a true experience of the New Testament believer-priests, we are.

Understanding Christ's rest

The Word says, "For he who has entered His rest has himself also ceased from his works as God did from His" (see Hebrews 4:10). As God rested from His completed work of creation, so Christ ceased from His finished work of redemption – and now rests! His work on behalf of humankind was accepted by God; He has entered into His rest and sits at the right hand of the Father on high.

By His example

In His earthly life, Jesus ceased from His own works and chose to live a complete life of dependence on His Father:

- I can of Myself do nothing (John 5:30).
- My doctrine is not Mine, but His who sent Me (John 7:16).
- The words that I speak to you I do not speak on My own authority; but the Father who dwells in Me does the work.

Jesus did not abandon this attitude of dependence until He had completed the last detail according to the pattern of His Father's plan. He then prayed,

"I have glorified you on the earth.
I have
Finished the work
You have given
Me to do."
– John 17:4

We have assurance that because Jesus has entered His rest – there remains a rest which we to can enter and enjoy. This truth is implied in v. 10, the believers will enter into their rest when they have finished their work for the kingdom of God on earth. We are told in Revelation 14:13, Then I heard a voice saying to me,

"Write Blessed are the dead who die in the Lord from now on."
"Yes," says the Spirit, that they may rest from their labors, and their
works follow them.

REFLECTION AND DISCUUSSION QUESTIONS: CHAPTER 4

1. All our fellowship and worship with God depends upon the activity of the _____ _____.

2. Discuss how the Old Testament offering provided a covering for sin.

3. To receive the righteousness and grace of Christ we must come to the _____.

4. Explain the biblical truth of "one way" to God.

5. Discuss and contrast God's rest of Creation, Christ's rest of redemption and the believer's rest.

6. I can apply this lesson to my life by:

7. Closing Statement of Commitment

SECTION III

The Righteousness of God

CHAPTER FIVE

Blending the Christian Faith

"God is a Spirit and those who worship Him
must worship in spirit and truth"
(John 4:24).

One of my focal points in the introduction of the tabernacle was the absence of Satan and the world in pure worship. They are absent because there is no place for them in this process of salvation which is of the Lord as we shall see in later chapters. Both are external and foreign to a true life of godliness. In other words, like the idol god [molded bull] brought out of Egypt with the children of Israel, not physically, but some of the Israelites brought the idle god along *in* their hearts (carefully study Exodus 32:1-35). Satan comes into the church when we leave an open space or vacuum in the people – today in the absence of love [agape], biblical knowledge, and denial of the Holy Spirit and His ministry Satan has moved in!

Moses was gone from the people for forty days, up in the Mount with God (see Ex. 24:18). Undoubtedly the way Moses departed and the forty days away caused many of the Israelites to grow impatient and began looking back to Egypt and the bull worshipped there. Along with Aaron, the high priest, they brought together their golden earrings; and Aaron fashioned the idol for them. Notice verse 4: Then they said, *"This is your god, O Israel that brought you out of the land of Egypt."* Thus, we see their attempt to **blend the worship** of the Lord with the symbolism of Baal, fertility gods and sacrifices combined with possible sexual acts of profane worship. Aaron willingly led the people in breaking the first three commandments:

- They bowed to another god besides the Lord.
- They made graven images.
- They used the Lord's name in false worship (see v. 5)

God had said repeatedly that it was He and He only who brought the Israelites out of Egypt (see Exodus 20:1, 2; 29:45, 46) an event they had all witnessed.

It is important that this passage be studied very carefully because the Israelites' worship of the golden calf reveals both the unfaithfulness of the Israelites and the great mercy of God [not giving them what they did deserve]. Even though the people had broken their promise to obey Him in such a short time, God forgave their sin and began again with them. It is important to note, eventually their cup of iniquity was full, and God had to send judgment.

I believe a great number of people in America believe that the grace and mercy of God wipes out their iniquity (sin), so "repentance and purity" are not an issue with them. Their worship simply turns into entertainment and their god, becomes themselves or their material goods. Folks! Life is not a gamble; and trying to live it without a right relationship with God and Christ is a no-win situation!

Only the blood of Jesus Christ washes away sin! The process begins with repentance [agreement with God's Word resulting in a complete turnaround with a changed mind]. We've got to make sure that we emphasize to our converts that salvation means:

1. More than simply believing,
2. But you must *understand* and *receive* a certain body of truth as *revealed* by the Holy Spirit and deliverance from the old sinful nature.
3. True worship happens only without sin [totally dependent upon God].

In their book, *Experiencing God,* Henry T. Blackaby and Claude V. King explain that the essence of sin is a shift from a God-centered life of total dependence to a self-centered life. Further, the essence of salvation is a denial of self and a return to God-centeredness, only then can God accomplish His purposes through us.[5]

Causing others to stumble

Satan will accept anyone's, or anything's help or any opportunity to pervert the true worship standards of God and disrupt the work of the Holy Spirit anywhere he possibly can. Aaron led the perverted worship service; and he was the high priest. Many of today's local churches are more concerned with programs and entertainment, numbers, comfort and building size than the righteousness of God through holy living, the operation of spiritual gifts, cultivating the fruit of the Spirit and the full ministry of the Holy Spirit.

Certainly, the absence of the Holy Spirit leaves the flock vulnerable for Satan's deceptions. In my book, *Manifestation of the True Children of God*, a major point I emphasize is, "One of the most deceptive practices in many of our churches today is the blanket acceptance of people who call themselves Christians, but claiming to be something and being it are two entirely different matters."[6] Dr. Billy Graham said, "Sleeping in the garage overnight does not make you and automobile." This is certainly a major cause of the growing dissension and lack of love, joy, and peace for many in the community of faith! The Scripture says,

> *"….. For the kingdom of God is not eating and drinking but righteousness, and joy and peace in the Holy Ghost"* (see Romans 14:17).

The kingdom of God does not consist of external things such as food, but in spiritual things like:

- Righteousness – in action, thought, conduct and behavior before others
- Peace – with God and man that seeks unity of the body
- Joy – of our salvation that comes only from the Holy Spirit

Many Christians undoubtedly forget that the kingdom of God is presently on earth and Christ is our King. We as the children of God are His loyal subjects. It is the King's will that we bear His image, display His righteousness, love, peace, and joy within us at all times, no matter the circumstances, those are the righteous acts of the saints [see Revelation 19:4], all for His witness and glory.

Now as kingdom kids, it is a serious thing to cause another brother or sister to stumble and fall into sin. In His discourse with the twelve, Jesus warned,

> *"But whoever causes one of these little ones who believe in Me to stumble, it would be better for him [or her] if a millstone were hung around his neck, and he was thrown into the sea. If your hand causes you to sin, cut it off. It is better for you to enter into life maimed,*

rather than having two hands, to go to hell, into the fire that shall never be quenched ...."(Mark 9:42-43).

In a day when the world considers everything "relative," many in the community of faith seem to be going along with the cultural flow. This trend is causing many to [*knowing the truth*] engage in commitments to sinful practices that automatically reject God and His moral law. When believers embrace immorality in any way or form it causes others to stumble, by their example [sins such as affairs, cohabitation, practicing same-sex relationships and marriages, heterosexuals committing themselves to remarriage even after unbiblical divorces]. You may ask me, why single out these sins? What about so and so? Committing such sins according to the Scriptures are abominations to God. These sins require "life choices" which affects our relationship with God – opening the door for Satan to pile on a lot of access baggage into your soul that you never would have imagined, such as:

1. A spirit of pride [I got away with it?]
2. The idea that God understands [me and my passions?]
3. Surely this is the exception [it's my time?]
4. Satan loves to advise, God forgives all sin – but what he does not explain or either you blindly refuse to see is that *forgiveness* requires *repentance* which brings about a complete about face, now that you see the error of your way and agree with God's Word on the sinful act, conduct, or behavior committed.

Satan's snares

In another section I discussed our sinful nature. Everyone knows from personal experiences in life that even though they are a Christian they continue to have the sinful nature in them (see Romans 7:32). Knowing that everyone is born with a sin nature, God's Word is very clear in warning against mixing with the world and its standards. Such sinful practices put the Christian on very unstable ground. Because when we mix with the world our sinful nature is tempted; and opens the door for spiritual activity.

Every believer should desire to do the will of God and follow His commands; yet the sincerest Christian knows how difficult that can be at times. That is especially true in our society where the influence it must teach is the self-centered way of the world.

Undoubtedly if you are a true believer and have fallen into Satan's snare, then fully fall on the grace and mercy of Christ:

- Acknowledge God's forgiveness and separate from the sin.
- Turn to Christ and seek Spiritual/ biblical pastoral counseling! Secular counseling is just that, the secular with secular conclusions and recommendations brought about through reason and science.

If the divorce is for reasons other than those found in Scripture – seek counseling. Many Christians are knowingly entering these life-long associations. The Word of God sets the standard and neither Hollywood nor the courts of the land can change them! The saints should understand that because a law is passed by our government that violates God's law – does not mean we are to support it.

You may be asking, "why these particular sins?" These practices are exceptions to orthodoxy and directly violate the truth of God's Word. Notice Jesus' reaction to the first record (see Genesis 18-19) of the effects of practiced homosexuality being endorsed in the culture (see Matthew 11:23-24; also, Jude 7).

Romans 1:26-27 gives us a clear New Testament passage on the verifiable consequences of sexual deviances from God's moral standards, **"changing the truth of God into a lie."** As a result, God gave them up to their own ways with devastating consequences – particularly this sin which is evidence of rebellion against God's design of all life *and rejection of the revealed Truth* of creation.

Please understand this is not about people who "fall off the wagon," and get up and get it right with God. This passage is referring to people who by their habitual sinful practices say to God, "I don't care what you say!" If you keep on reading in this passage, you'll notice that homosexuality was only one of the issues that Paul was speaking to. Paul recorded a long list of habitual, sinful practices that give evidence that the Holy Spirit does not reside in the lives of those committing such. Many of these people who are in sin did not fall, but jumped.

- Anyone holding on to their questionable practices and causes another Christian to fall in their walk with God is spiritually blind to the price Jesus paid on the cross for sin.
- Our good should never be of that which causes evil talk. After all, as stated above, the Christian life is not a matter of eating

or drinking (or any other practice), but one of righteousness and peace and joy in the Holy Spirit.

- Our goal should not be to please ourselves, but to glorify God and edify [build up] others in the body of Christ – in love!

In 1 Corinthians 10:23, Paul states that all things are lawful for the believer, but not everything builds up or helps to build up others. How selfish it is for a Christian to tear down a fellow believer's spiritual life because of his or her own selfish living. Even though their practices may be lawful – they do not come under the law of love.

If he or she has seen anything in the Word of God and concludes that they have liberty in the matter, he or she should still not exercise Christian liberty to allow it to become an occasion for a weaker brother or sister to stumble. If you practice something that is not sinful but may nevertheless offend others, don't make an issue of it.

Through religion, academia, Islam, human secularism, multiculturalism, the media, partisan politics, spiritual and biblical illiteracy, coupled with the various sinful practices and conditions that I have mentioned above are seeping into the body of Christ in an attempt to blend with Christianity; therefore across this land we have the hybrid of a pseudo-Christianity parading as the norm. Some pastors read from both the Holy Bible and the Koran in their worship services. Others have blended Christian practice with Islam [Chrislam]. It indicates conformity on a grand scale, because of the *"lack of Spiritual and biblical knowledge of the truth."*

- Research shows that some churches are rejecting the blood of Jesus and the Holy Spirit's gifts and ministry as no longer necessary in their forms of godliness.
- We are noticing today that some Christian Communities are assimilating sinners by allowing them to join their churches with the expectation that they will accept Christ and be saved at some later date.
- The old sacred hymns of the church are either rejected totally or in many cases blended with secular thoughts and non-spiritual moves [called "rocking"].
- Others are receiving people into membership based upon their talents, material goods, secular experiences, positions, and earthly power, yet they are not born again.

- Local churches have the right to establish standards, but not beyond what the Word of God teaches. Some churches are going so far as to change their constitutions and by-laws to accommodate sins of the flesh as if that changes God's moral law. All supposedly in the name of love and compassion and so-called political correctness.

- Today many are creating their own gods, by denying the fact that Moses' God of the Old Testament and Jesus' God of the New Testament is one and the same God. Though the Mosaic Law has passed away; God's Moral Law is eternal.

As we noted in Chapter 2, to enter the holy place the priest could have no unconfessed or unjudged sins in their lives [believers today face the same standards] for fellowship with God and Christ. God has made provision for this condition in 1 John 1:9, but like Romans 10:9-10, many times it is either overlooked or substituted by some illogical blend of false teaching.

Our own fellowship with God and Christ was non-existent until we were "born from above" by the Holy Spirit. Until a person is crucified with Christ [set apart by the blood of His sacrifice] which is typified by the sacrifice on the brazen altar there is no journey for them to the brazen laver, and definitely not into the holy place for fellowship and worship with the Lord. Seeing this picture, many still consider what they are doing to be acceptable to God. It is time to stop and examine ourselves, and make sure we are in the truth of God's Word.

So many Christians have believed on Christ, but have bogged themselves down in carnality somewhere between the brazen altar and the brazen laver, still on the milk of the Word years after confessing Christ because they for whatever reason can't "eat meat" and grow into a deeper spiritual life. Of course, this is as for as any church can carry their members if they are operating through "science and reason" rather than, biblically operating through the Holy Spirit's gifts and ministry.

Jesus Christ is the only way to God!

Be holy for I am holy! The Scripture says, God is a Spirit and those who worship Him must do so in spirit and in truth (John 4:24). We know that the unsaved are alienated from God because of sin inherited from Adam, yet many are allowed to substitute talent, family, numbers and entertainment for the content of true worship. It is unfair to continue leading the people to believe that mixed seed is acceptable to God.

True worship is spiritual and totally impossible unless you have been *regenerated* by the Holy Spirit. Like the Philippian jailer in Acts 16:30, you may be asking, *"What must I do to be saved?"* Paul and Silas said, *"Believe on the Lord Jesus Christ, and you will be saved"* (Acts 16:31; also, carefully study John 3:6; Romans 10:9-10). The promise remains valid today.

"Believe on the Lord Jesus Christ and you will be saved."

Apart from the Holy Spirit "regeneration" is totally impossible!

Regeneration

Regeneration or ["born from above" see John 3:3-6] begins as our spirit which was spiritually dead due to sin inherited from Adam is quickened [brought to life] by God, the Holy Spirit, once the individual hears and receives the gospel of Jesus Christ.

Figure 2

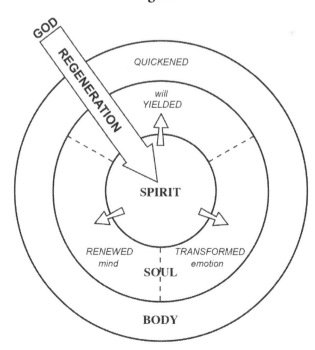

This is the results of the Spirit drawing and convicting us of our sins, [sinful nature] followed by our true repentance and acceptance of Jesus Christ as your personal Lord and Savior [see Figure #2 above]. At which time, we are reconciled to God by grace through faith in the finished work of our Lord and Savior, Jesus Christ alone (see Isaiah 53:11; Romans 10:9-10; 14:16-17, 26).

Please notice the arrows in [Figure #2 above], our now born-again spirit is exerting pressure outwardly to renew our soul and body. In regeneration our old Adamic nature is exchanged for a divine nature. Now that the Holy Spirit has entered the individual, He abides taking up residence and begins the process of transformation wherein the soul which consists of [the mind which is renewed through the *revealed* truths of God's Word]. The body following is quickened [made alive] by the Spirit.

Three groups of humans

The Apostle Paul has divided all of humanity into three groups: (1) the "natural man" – who is unsaved or unchanged spiritually; (2) the "carnal man" – who is a babe in Christ and walks "as a man" (3) the "spiritual man, who walks with God."

Paul classifies these groups according to their ability to *understand* and *receive* <u>a particular body of Truth</u> consisting of things *revealed* unto us by the Holy Spirit. Human beings are distinguished from one another by:

- The fact of the new birth from above
- The deeper life of power and blessing

The reality of either of the two is determined by the attitude of the individual toward the things revealed. In 1 Corinthians 2:9-3:4, the three-fold difference is made clear as follows. But as it is written,

> *"Eye has not seen, nor ear heard, nor have entered the heart of man, the things which God has prepared for those who love Him. But God has revealed them to us through His Spirit"* (1 Corinthians 2:9-10a).

These words from Isaiah 64:4, refers to the wisdom God has prepared for His true believer-priests. It is impossible for anyone to be able to discover by eye or ear [empirical evidence], nor can it be found by the mind [subjective, *rational* conclusions].

The wisdom that saves a person – human wisdom *cannot know, it is revealed by God.*

He makes it known by revelation, inspiration, and illumination:

- Revelation was given to those who wrote the Bible (see vv. 10-11).
- Inspiration and illumination are given to all believers who seek to know and understand the divinely written body of Truth (vv. 12-16).
- But in each case, please know – the Holy Spirit is the divine agent doing the work through the Scriptures, only the Holy Spirit *reveals* the truth of God's Word, for us through inspiration and illumination (see 2 Peter 1:21).

The deep things of God

In the last section we saw that Paul classified human beings as in one of three groups; and each group is determined by our ability to understand and receive the "deep things of God." We will go into more details on the three groups later. The Scripture continues,

"For the Spirit searches all things, yes, the deep things of God. For what man knows the things of a man except the spirit of the man which is in him? Even so no one knows the things of God except the Spirit of God" (1 Corinthians 2:10b-11).

I think the Holy Spirit's intention is to impress upon you, the reader, that:

- No one unaided by the Spirit of God can understand and receive the "deep things of God."
- Without the Holy Spirit a person can enter freely into the things of his or her fellow human beings, because of the human spirit which is in them.
- However, a person cannot extend their sphere to know experimentally the animal kingdom below nor enter a higher sphere and experimentally know the things of God.

Even though humans of themselves cannot know the things of God, the Spirit knows them, and a person may be so related to the Spirit that he or she may also know them.

The Scripture continues,

> *"Now we have received,*
> *not the spirit of the world,*
> *but the Spirit who is from God,*
> *that we might know*
> *the things that have*
> *been freely given to us by God"*(v. 12).

Again, we could never know "the things that are freely given to us of God," however, the Spirit knows, and He indwells us, and He *reveals* them to us through the Word of God, [the sword of the Spirit]. Praise God!

The sword of the Spirit

In Ephesians 6:10-18, the Apostle Paul admonishes the saints, *"Finally, my brethren, be strong in the Lord and in the power of His might. Put on the whole armor of God that you may be able to stand against the wiles of the devil. For we do not, wrestle against flesh and blood, but against principalities, against powers, against the rulers of darkness of this age, against spiritual hosts of wickedness in the heavenly places. Therefore, take up the whole armor of God that you may be able to withstand in the evil day, and having done all, to stand." Stand therefore,*

- *Having girded your waist with truth,*
- *Having put on the breastplate of righteousness,*
- *Having shod your feet with the preparation of the gospel of peace*
- *Above all, taking the shield of faith with which, you will be able to quench all the fiery darts of the wicked one,*
- *And take the helmet of salvation,*
- *And* **the sword of the Spirit, which is the Word of God.**

The sword of the Spirit is the only offensive weapon in the believer's armor. It is [the Bible], the only piece of spiritual armor that is tangible and seen with the physical eye. Notice the other five pieces are spiritual and remain in the unseen spiritual realm. God brought the Bible out of the unseen spiritual realm and made it physically available to all. To have the precise word at the ready, the Christian must know the Word of God intimately. "Put on" conveys the idea of permanence, indicating that armor should be the Christian's sustained life-long attire. The whole matter of spiritual warfare is the be bathed in prayer. The Scripture admonishes, "praying always with all prayer and supplication in the Spirit" (v. 18). "Always" means all begins and ends in prayer, which is a spiritual warfare. We are to focus our prayer on submitting to the will of God.

The divine revelation

The divine revelation is communicated to us in "words" by the Holy Spirit who teaches us. Paul states, *"Which things also we speak, not in words which man's wisdom teaches, but which the Holy Spirit teaches, comparing spiritual with spiritual.* Human words are used to convey "human wisdom," however, only Spiritual revelation conveys the things which *"eye has not seen, nor ear heard, neither have entered into the heart of man."*

Nevertheless, without the Holy Spirit's enablement humans cannot understand these "deep things of God," though couched in words most familiar to people, except they are *revealed* by the Spirit. Understanding comes only through comparing one spiritual thing with another spiritual thing. Apart from the Holy Spirit there can be no spiritual understanding.

"Without the Holy Spirit there can be no spiritual understanding!"

The meat of the matter

Many of the local churches are laden with hypocrisy, compromise, internal pains, unsolved problems, and a lack of true spiritual life mainly because of the lack of missional priorities in the church. Such churches become dull, lifeless, and predictable. They display more reverence for their own religious traditions than for essential biblical truth. Many local churches care so much about numbers until Satan has little difficulty planting his counterfeits; to display their superficial manner among the members with little if any real involvement in each other's lives. Everybody is in the process of either salvation or the process of destruction. How we respond to the finished work of Jesus Christ determines where we stand. Therefore, in 1 Corinthians 3:1-7, the apostle Paul classified everyone in the membership of the church as either natural, carnal or spiritual.

The differences among these groups have continuously caused divisions since the early church. Many churches are losing their spirituality by striving to be inclusive of people who defiantly live in open rebellion against God and Christ, some are regenerated and some unregenerate as some local churches assimilate themselves with the relativistic culture. As we look at these groups, we can see that only a third of them have a clear revelation of Christ and His finished work on the Cross. It's obvious that the goal of discipleship (spiritual maturity) will not be a concern in this church. Again, notice the three below:

- *The natural man* is unregenerate with a dead human spirit inherited from Adam's sin nature. This person has no appreciation for the gospel it is foolishness to them; nor do the unregenerate have the ability to receive the Spirituality of Christ because they have not been "born again from above" (see 2:14; John 3:3).
- *The carnal Christian* must be fed with "milk" and not with "solid food" (see 3:2), so therefore he or she will not find the wisdom of the Holy Spirit given only to those fully yielded to Christ. This Christian is not fully yielded and walking in the Spirit (study carefully Romans 8:1-16). This happens when we commit to Spiritual growth through personal prayer, study and meditation of the Word and allow the Holy Spirit to reveal the deeper truths of God's Word.
- *The Spiritual Christian* through the revelation and wisdom of the deeper life in the Spirit, without which the divisions and lack of unity in the church cannot be solved. This wisdom is not from academic achievement but received from above. Allowing place to the flesh diminishes the capacity in your human spirit for the Holy Spirit to mature you to full discipleship.

It's important to note once again, the unregenerate sinner can only live a life of sin. But the regenerated Christian can live both lives, but not at the same time.

Be of one mind [wisdom from above]

Paul offers several suggestions to the Corinthians:

1. *Strive for wider cooperation among Christians.* (3:5-9)
   Paul and Apollos had "one mind" as they worked together. Paul
   sowed the seed in Corinth, and Apollos watered it (3:6).They
   rejoiced when God gave the increase. Others came together
   in groups with their eyes on a person – some wanted to follow
   Apollos, others Paul and some Christ, rather than speak with one
   mind.

2. *Have full confidence in the work of the Holy Spirit.* (3:5-9)
   Once a person is born again, he or she receives the ministry of
   the Holy Spirit in their heart. How effective the Spirit's work is in
   us is dependent upon our giving up the flesh.

   We are to allow the Holy Spirit's total control; our spiritual
   growth [maturity] depends on it. If we allow the attitude of "one
   mind" and under the Holy Spirit's full control of our lives will
   eliminate divisions very quickly.

3. *Stop judging you brother in Christ.* (3:10-15, 18-21)
   Finally, Paul suggests to the Corinthians that they stop judging
   their brothers in Christ. He inserts the passage on the Judgment
   Seat of Christ to remind the Corinthians that each Christian is
   responsible before God for his or her own acts. Since God will
   judge each individual according to his or her works, Christians
   should stop taking upon themselves God's prerogative of
   judgment. Paul exhorts, *"So do not pass premature judgment before
   the Lord comes"* (5:5).

How to handle church divisions?

- Look behind whatever superficial reasons are given and locate the
  carnality that certainly is there.
- Carnal Christians with their worldly attitudes are always behind
  divisions in the church.
- Each of us has the responsibility to heal the divisions and strive to
  prevent the occurrence of new ones.

- Carnality plays funny tricks. Notice the Corinthians divided when they were supposed to be one; and they remained together when they should have been divided.

Carnality's great deception

In chapters 5 and 6 of First Corinthians, Paul faces a different challenge, but once again carnality is the cause. An adulterous affair between a man and his stepmother becomes known (see 5:1). This sin was even frowned upon by the non-believing Gentiles. Although the sin shocked Paul deeply, it was not the most serious sin. Even worse than this sin, was the apparent arrogant attitude of the whole congregation toward this immorality.

> *"And you, rather than grieving about it enough to remove the person who committed such a deed, are you puffed up?"*(5:2)

The carnality seen here is so prevalent in churches today; because of it the Christians had allowed "pride" to creep into their hearts concerning this sin. In (5:6), Paul labeled it "boasting." What were they proud of? Their pride centered in their concept of "tolerance." They prided themselves it seems with being able to absorb or live with the situation? Many leaders today explain away such sin rationally:

- What the brother does in his private life is not our concern.
- He tithes and attends church regularly; those are the minimum requirements for being in good standing here.
- Furthermore, this affair with his stepmother is probably wholesome and meaningful for both.
- Let's not be pharisaical about this!
- We are obligated to continue to love him [what's happening here?]

Undoubtedly excommunicating either of them was never a consideration; as if to say, "Don't rock the boat!" When such sin is tolerated it will permeate and damage the whole church. Watch and pray for your church. Not to apply discipline when necessary reflects carnality in the leadership as the above case indicates.

It is quite evident that the Holy Spirit, nor His ministry or the Word of God was a priority in this case. Such conduct has almost become the norm **today, but to tolerate such behavior does not help anyone,** especially those involved in the affair or other inappropriate conduct and behavior. Watch and pray for your church beginning with your leaders. Paul insisted on strict discipline and admonishes, **"Purge out the old leaven ...."** (v.7).The church is in the world but not of the world.

Who are we to judge?

In America today we seem to think nothing of being faithful in our daily Bible reading even injecting our opinion in our Bible-study group, after all we believe in truth, but very subtlety the secular worldview has invaded the Christian conversation to a point today wherein many in the church are agreeing with the world and sinking deeper into the cultural norms. The culture in these United States firmly believes that truth and morality are *relative.*

We believe, or say we believe, that all people have a right to their own opinion – that is except those who hold that some opinions are better than others. Academia's culture holds to the tenets of moral relativism while at the same time marginalizing those who apparently *violate* its rules against:

- Insensitivity
- Intolerance members
- Political correctness
- Morality

Our headlines are filled with ethical, moral, and social issues from abortion to physician-assisted suicide, to same-sex marriages to cohabitation to animal-human equality. Unfortunately, even in our churches, many seem to assume that *rational discussion* has no place in the conflicts over moral questions and that no answers to such questions exist. In other words, to them we are simply stuck with, "our opinions are relative."

Relativism has landed

Relativism is the theory that "there is no objective standard by which truth may be determined – so truth varies with individuals and circumstances.[7]

We know that relativism is theory and like the theory of evolution, it has been accepted and taught as truth. In other words, these lies, and their very harmful consequences are preferable for a growing segment of our society over the all-loving, all-wise, and all-knowing God and Creator of the universe and all therein. Our public school's textbooks and the texts our colleges, universities, libraries and curricula have been rewritten to internalize and institutionalize these deceptive lies. Today we are witnessing a generation that has internalized moral relativism.

Over the past several years we have witnessed their fruit in the decision-making processes of all branches of our government, academia the news media and even some Christian communities. More and more people are accepting them as being true because that's all that most of them have been offered. Like the prodigal, this nation has found itself in the pigpen, but unlike him – the pigpen seems to be preferable according to our present national state and condition than the Father's house (see Luke 15:11-23).

Believing a lie

Acceptance of these theories is the results of a determined effort to replace God, His moral standards, and absolute truth. What is sad about this whole mess is the fact that many members of this generation have never heard the gospel of Christ or the *true* truth about Creation. Sadly, the most subtle and rewarding goal of much of the emerging generations today is simply their "personal happiness" and "their stuff" which justifies any means they may chose to attain that self-serving end [study Romans 1:1-21]. Perhaps we should examine moral relativism a little closer. It is relativism applied to the morals of a society. What is a society? Webster's Dictionary defines a society as:

- A voluntary association of persons for common ends.
- A part of a community bound together by common interests and standards.

I don't think the implications of where all of this is leading have fully sunk in with many pastors and other church leaders yet. The Scriptures speak of the "doctrines of demons" (see 1Timothy 4:1). Satan and his demons will speak the truth if it serves their purpose to deceive. Some of the theories taught as nothing but theories fifty to sixty years ago are now being taught as truth – at the expense of God's Word of Truth.

Because morality is reduced to personal tastes, people exchange the moral question: What is good? With the pleasure question: What feels good? When self-interests rules, it profoundly impacts behavior, especially how we treat other people:

- If there is no truth, then nothing has transcendent value, including human beings.
- Human dignity and respect depend on the existence of moral truth.
- Without human dignity there is no obligation of self-sacrifice on behalf of others.
- It becomes easy to just "kick some one to the curb" when they become a burden, expensive or begin to cramp our lifestyle.
- When people are viewed as things, they begin to be treated as things.
- Gruesome newscasts compete with prime time shows, because many of them have become mere entertainment.
- For some reason many in society think they can have it both ways, but that cannot happen. The courts and governmental choices are being made for various reasons without considering God's moral laws and values only becoming more satanic!
- No longer will we allow a hint of moral censure on sexual practices that were regarded as perverse only one generation ago.
- Despite all the collateral damage to our institutions; America's pride in our tolerance is like the Corinthians of old – yet tolerate absolutely no one who doesn't adhere [agree] to its moral open-mindedness.
- We should also note carefully that the notion of *offendedness* is highly emotional in character and is showing itself in many devious ways today: public schools, church, marriage and family violence, rape and child abuse, home invasions, road rage, drive by crimes, workplace violence, daily mass killings and the recently acknowledged home-grown terrorists in this country – are just a few examples.
- In other words, those who now claim to be offended are in an emotional state that has resulted from contact with someone else's belief system.

Today our society has witnessed a cultural shift in the meaning of "offend" and all that is required [to set people off is] the vaguest notion of emotional dissatisfaction at what another has said, done or presented. Now the "right never to be offended" is not only accepted as legitimate but is promoted by the media, academia, government, various activists and other special interest groups. How are the Christians to treat all of this? Well, Church history reports that under similar and eventually worse circumstances the early Christians turned the world upside down!

Given the command from Christ, our Savior to,

Go therefore and make disciples of all nations, baptizing them in the name of the Father and of the Son and of the Holy Spirit, teaching them to observe all things that I have commanded you; and lo, I am with you always, even to the end of the age" (Matthew 28:19, 20).

We are to share the Gospel and witness openly and publicly about Jesus

Christ, our Lord and Savior, and our Christian faith. As Christians, we must clearly understand our responsibility to protect *free speech* and resist this culture of offendedness that threatens to shut down all public discourse.

Speaking publicly about Jesus Christ is the Christian's right, which means that those of other belief systems will be equally free to present their truth claims in an equally public manner.

This is the cost of religious freedom. As the Apostle Paul made clear in the writing to the Corinthians, the preaching of the gospel has always been considered *offensive* by those who reject it. When Paul spoke of the Cross as "foolishness" to the Greeks and a "stumbling block" to the Jews (see 1 Corinthians 1:23), he was pointing to this very reality – a reality that would eventually lead to his own stoning, imprisonment, and gruesome execution.

Paul did not want to offend people based on anything other than the cross of Jesus Christ and the essentials of the Christian faith. For that reason, he would write to the Corinthians about becoming,

"All things to all people,
that by all means I might save other."
I Corinthians 9:22

The truth claims of Christianity, by their peculiarity, and exclusivity are inherently *offensive* to those who would demand some other gospel (see Galatians 3:1).

To our shame and certainly to the injury of our own testimony some Christians manage to be offensive for reasons other than the gospel. However, there is absolutely no way for a faithful Christian to avoid offending those who are offended by Jesus Christ and His finished work on the cross.

REFLECTION AND DISCUSSION QUESTIONS: CHAPTER 5

1. Discuss what prompted the people to desire idol gods while Moses was in the mount with God?

2. Discuss why there is no mention of Satan and the world in the tabernacle worship?

3. Explain true "repentance" and its part in the salvation process.

4. Discuss how you are to handle something you practice which is not sinful, but offends a brother?

5. The Scripture says, "God is Spirit and those who worship Him must do so in _____ and _____.

6. I can apply this lesson to my life by:

7. Closing Statement of Commitment

CHAPTER SIX

Stay Connected

"You are already clean because of the Word, which I have spoken to you. Abide in Me and I in you, as the branch cannot bear fruit of itself, unless it abides in the vine, neither can you, unless you abide in Me" (John 15:3-4).

One of the major truths that I'm striving to drive home in this book is "you are cleansed through the Word." Cleansed means there are no unconfessed sins in your life. Looking into the mirror [a type] of God's Word (see James 1:23-25), at the brazen laver and confessing typifies the believer today looking into the mirror of the Word. If we detect unconfessed sin – we must repent and confess it, then take appropriate corrective action which might include making restitution.

Confession

One day I heard a preacher say, "I go out in my daily walk and sin, but I come to the brazen altar which parallels the cross asking for forgiveness and go on boldly to the throne of grace for my help. What that preacher expressed that day is so sad because that is where we find most believers today. With this gross misunderstanding they are hanging out somewhere between the brazen altar and the brazen laver in confusion and unbelief. Some people come to the brazen laver [the Word of God] daily and instead of obeying the direction of the Word through the Spirit and confessing; they retreat in unbelief. The Scripture says,

"If we confess our sins, He is faithful and just to forgive us our sins and to cleanse us from all unrighteousness" (1 John 1:9).

In spite of knowing and believing the truth, many spend their life dashing back and forth between the foot of the cross and the brazen laver;

their minds flooded with unbelief and access baggage supplied by the media or perhaps guilt of something the devil has dug up from their past. As I said in an earlier section, any form of disobedience or continuing in sin can construct an impregnable barrier preventing our being able to reach the presence of God (carefully study Isaiah 59:2; Psalm 66:18). It is good to be reminded:

- We can never come to God in disobedience to His commandments.
- We cannot approach God, whether in prayer or praise, supplication or intercession, except through Christ by the Holy Spirit.
- Even though we have the right of access we are still required to come with clean hands and a pure heart into God's presence.
- Only by the confession of known sin, and renunciation of it does the death of Christ and the power of His blood avail itself for us to draw near to God.
- We should never act or pray contrary to the will of God.

As children of God, the New Testament does not encourage us to continue wandering around in sin due to our spiritual and biblical illiteracy of the truths of God's Word; it emphasizes the need of being filled with:

- The knowledge of His will – by increasing "in the knowledge of God" (see Colossians 1:9).
- Understanding what the will of the Lord is – "Be filled with the Holy Spirit" (see Ephesians 5:17).
- Proving what is the will of God – through a "renewed mind" (see Romans 12:2).

The apostle John assures us,

> *"Now this is the confidence*
> *that we have in Him,*
> *that if we ask anything*
> *according to His will,*
> *He hears us.*
> *And if we know that*
> *He hears us*
> *whatever we ask,*

we know that we have the petitions
that we have asked Him for"
1 John 5:14-15

SPECIAL NOTE: The key to knowing that God hears our prayers is to pray according to His will. We know His will by His Spirit and His Word.

This phrase "according to His will" presents a definite key to answered prayer. To pray according to His will is to pray in accordance with His desires; not what we would desire or insist that He does for us (see John 14:13-14).

Hopefully true believers know God's Word [His will] and practice those things that are pleasing to Him and:

- They never insist on their own will, but God's will be the priority (see Matthew 26:39-42).
- The Scripture assures us that God always hears the prayers of His children, but not always in the manner they were presented (see Psalm 34:15-17).
- Jesus commands, "That we abide in Him and His Word abide in us and ask what we will, and it shall be done for us" (see John 15:7).

Abide in Me

The word "abide" means to remain, to dwell or to stay connected. Jesus' teaching in the parable of the connection between the vine and the branch is a living union. This union is not the work of man, but of God. The union demonstrates the life, sap, and the fruitfulness that the vine transmits to the branch – so it is with the true believer and Christ also. The union of the believer and his or her Lord is not the results of human wisdom or human performance, but an act of Almighty God; whereby the most complete life-union is instituted between the Son of God and the sinner.

God sent forth the Holy Spirit into the hearts of believers. The same Spirit becomes the life of the believer in the unity of one Spirit and the *fellowship* of the same life which is in Christ makes the believer one with Him. Just as between the vine and its branches, the life-union makes them one.

The completeness of the union

We see in Jesus' teaching of the vine and branches the completeness of the union and each is nothing without the other – the vine owes its right to life and fruitfulness to the vineyard. So, the Lord says, "Without me you can do nothing." The believer can be pleasing each day to God only in what he or she does through Christ who strengthens them.

The daily inflowing of the life-sap of the Holy Spirit is the believer's only power to bring forth fruit as he or she is each moment dependent upon Him alone. A vine without branches cannot bear fruit. Neither can the branch bear fruit without the vine. In His grace of condescension Jesus, said, "Just as His people are dependent on Him, He has made Himself dependent on them."

Therefore, without His true followers Christ cannot dispense His blessing to the world. Nor can He offer sinners the fruit of heaven. Christ's redeemed ones are indispensable to Him on earth; it's through them that His fruit may be found. What a glorious privilege and responsibility we have in serving our Lord. Certainly, considering His love and what He has done for us – His will should always be our first concern.

In 1 Corinthians 13:4-7, Paul admonishes the brethren concerning some of the practical aspects of the spirit of love as it ought to manifest itself in the Christian fellowship in Christ in the Church at Corinth through a series of verbs. And like many local churches today in the body of Christ the church was not perfect but had the potential to be great. Spiritual gifts were operating in the church, yet these fractious brethren should be a guide to us in dealing with faith communities in our own day.

It is love that gives its value to any gift of the spirit; it is love for Christ and the brethren that sanctifies the Christian in the cause. Paul does not define love, but he goes to great length to tell his readers how it works; he is anxious for them to follow God's way of life:

- The way that never fails
- The way that leads straight to God's predestined goal
- The way of love!

The way of love

The Scripture says, "God is love." That is not saying that God has love or love is a characteristic of God, but it says, "God is love." In the same way the Holy Spirit, Himself, is the "power of God." The way of love then says, we are "love" individually and corporately. If love is lacking in me, then I am nothing. In fact, it's only a matter of time before I will be a disgrace to the kingdom of God, trying to represent God without love. However, in 1 Corinthians 13:4-7 in the same manner as a true child of God in Christ, I am the embodiment of:

1. Love suffers long [deal with difficult people].
2. Love is kind [a loving smile and manner for all people].
3. Love does not envy [help others to excel].
4. Love does not parade itself [greatly aware of their importance in their own eyes].
5. Love does not behave rudely [arrogant and proud].
6. Love does not seek its own [it's my way or the highway attitude].
7. Love is not provoked [irritable].
8. Love thinks no evil [mind on things above].
9. Love does not rejoice in iniquity [does not harbor memories of wrongs personally suffered].
10. Love rejoices in the truth [loves the revealed truth of God's Word].
11. Love bears all things [takes upon itself the sins and failures of others].
12. Love believes all things [believes the best about people].
13. Love hopes all things [continues to hope for the best even if for the time it can find no adequate grounds for such hope].
14. Love endures all things [where there is no ground for hope love endures].

This love [Gk. Agape] in the New Testament took on a special meaning – it is a volitional love as opposed to the purely emotional kind. It is a sacrificial love, a kind naturally expressed by God but not so easily by people. In fact, it is only characteristic of the people of God. Therefore,

"Seek first the kingdom of God and His righteousness, and all these things shall be added to you" (see Matthew 6:33).

REFLECTION AND DISCUSSION QUESTIONS: CHAPTER 6

1. Any form of disobedience or continuing in sin can construct an impregnable barrier preventing our reaching the _____ of God.

2. Discuss the teaching of the parable of the vine and the branches and how the life-union makes them one; relate the discussion to the union with Christ.

3. In His condescension, just as His people are dependent on Him, He made Himself dependent on them to dispense His grace to the world. In your estimation how are we doing?

4. Discuss Jesus' words, "You are cleansed through the Word."

5. We should never act or pray contrary to the _____ of _____.

6. I can apply this lesson to my life by:

7. Closing Statement of Commitment.

SECTION IV

The Plumb Line

CHAPTER SEVEN

Two Ways of Life

*"But we all, with unveiled faces, beholding as in a mirror the
glory of the Lord, are being transformed into the same image
from glory to glory, just as by the Spirit of the Lord"*
(2 Corinthians 3:18).

*"And do not be conformed to this world, but be transformed
by the renewing of your mind, that you may prove what is
that good and acceptable and perfect will of God"*
(Romans 12:2).

Earlier we saw that the mirror is a symbol of God's Word in which
we not only see ourselves, but we see the Son of God. As we worship Him
and behold His glory – we are *transformed* by His Word and the Spirit
to share in His image and glory. We reveal His increasing glory causing
others to see Christ in us and honor Him (see Proverbs 4:18). We become
like the God we worship (see Psalm 115:8).

We are what? [Transformed or Conformed]

As we worship the true God in spirit and in truth, we are transformed
to become more like Him. Now to answer the question above, what we
are and what we do are both determined by our worship:

Transformed

Paul is responsible for revealing to us how we arrive there. He
instructs that we are involved in a crisis of *dedication* as he recorded in
Romans 12:1-2 and in 2 Corinthians 3:18; a process of *transformation*.
Both dedication and transformation work in tandem with each other
as we:

- Yield our body, mind, and will to the Lord, while studying, meditating and internalizing the truths of His Word.
- The Spirit of God transforms us into *"living sacrifices"* with "renewed minds" reflecting the glory of God.
- It is no longer I – but Christ! This transformation was prophesied in the Old Testament by Ezekiel:

"I will give you a new heart and put a new spirit in you; I will remove from you your heart of stone and give you a heart of flesh. And I will put My Spirit in you" (Ezekiel 36:26-27).

The prophet Jeremiah prophesied, *"I will put My law in their minds and write it on their hearts"* (Jeremiah 31:33).

When you became a believer, you became a new person in Christ Jesus. Your process of transformation began – not because of anything you have done or could have done, but of what Christ accomplished on the cross for us. As I've pointed out several times in this book, Christ became our righteousness – opening the door for each true believer to have a life-changing relationship with God. That's what it means to be "in Christ."

"In Christ" is not some religious feeling. It is not an emotional experience. It is entering into the reality of Christ's work. Jesus said, "This ...... is the new covenant in My blood" (see Luke 22:20). Please notice, the kind of experience that we have been talking about:

- beholding the glory of God in the Word
- seeing the Son of God in the Word

And afterward we are transformed by the Spirit, into salt and light, reflectors of God's glory, carrying the gospel of the kingdom to the world in our daily lives. This experience demands *devotion* and *discipline*. Consider the moon and the stars and the light *reflected* across the universe through them, neither has the ability nor power to produce the light that stretches amongst the billions of stars, in fact neither has any light of its own. Where does the light reflected by them come from? The *sun!*

Likewise, as transformed true believer-priests produce absolutely no light of their own, but through the power of the Holy Spirit the path of the transformed is one of increasing light. Like a sunrise the transformed begins with the faint glow of dawn and proceeds to the splendor of noonday radiating and reflecting the glorious light of the *Son* of God to light the world:

"But the path of the just is like the shining sun,
That shines ever brighter
unto the perfect day"
– Proverbs 4:18

Many would probably consider the devotion, but very few these days are interested in the discipline. However, to be useful and transformed believers both are required. Paul admonished Timothy to exercise himself to godliness (see 1Timothy 4:7, 8). This suggests that today's believers need the same kind of discipline exercised by successful athletes. Perhaps we can begin by balancing our time spent on spiritual things and Christian development with equal time that we give to sports, TV, hobbies, and our golf game. "Am I willing to pay the price that will please God and accomplish His purpose for my life?"

The Christian consensus has for the most part been replaced with the secular consensus today in the Western World. Sooner or later some legislators will decide that Christianity is only about what happens inside the church buildings. We have a responsibility to defend the faith – by remaining true to and sharing our beliefs with others – just as members of various other faiths and nonbelievers should be free to do.

We enter the Church to worship but leave to serve in the world. Defending our faith is not about forcing our beliefs on others, as the progressives charge. We must stand and speak up clearly and be obedient in representing our Lord well in the world. Therefore, it is highly possible that many of us may become martyrs as the world grows weaker and the consensus of the ungodly grows darker. The Scripture speaks of a time when men will kill you and think they are doing God a favor.

I watched a PBS documentary some time ago on the KKK and I was shocked at their filmed church service, the prayers, sermons and songs seemed to have all been done very sincerely in the name of Jesus, and that was frightening because they were just as sincere in their comments about their hatred for non-whites and Jews, superiority of the white race, and their claim that this country was established for whites only.

In another room a couple of women were indoctrinating the smaller children by openly planting hatred for other races. There was absolutely no doubt in my mind that they really believed that Jesus Christ was on their side.

If we are being persecuted for the sake of Christ and the earthly expansion of His kingdom; then so be it! When transformed

Christ-bearers of biblical truth show up in any crowd of those who prefer conformity – it's sad to say most of the people automatically feel threatened by our presence. Why?

- The glory of God in our lives is both permanent and increasingly more glorious.
- When Moses worshipped God on the mount, upon returning to the camp his face shone from the glory of God's presence which was external and temporary therefore he put a veil over his face to hide the fading glory from the people (see Exodus 34:29-35).
- Through the process of transformation by the Spirit, those who are in Christ inwardly receive an increase of the glory of God. Instead of veiling our faces, we want the world to see what the grace of God can do in the life of the true child of God. Let us boldly stand and "Let the light from the Lighthouse [Christ] shine" in and through us:

"But we all, with unveiled face, beholding as in a mirror the glory of the Lord, are being transformed into the same image from glory to glory, just as by the Spirit of the Lord" (2 Corinthians 3:18).

For those in Christ the only acceptable worship is to offer themselves completely to the Lord. When the Holy Spirit comes into the born-again human spirit – He makes that spirit holy. Only then is He readily able to renew the unredeemed soul and body through the individual's new divine nature. The Whole being [person] must be yielded to Christ as an instrument of light and righteousness "walking circumspectly" before a dying world (see Romans 6:12, 13; 8:11-13).

Conformed and Transformed contrasted

Paul also instructed that along with the transformed in the church, there would be the conformed, those who are shaped and conformed to the world's standards [carnal or worldly Christians]. These folks live so close to the edge that you can hardly tell them from the unsaved.

- The transformed trust God to do His work as they worship, pray, and sow the seed of God's Word; at the same time the conformed seek new techniques as they attempt to do God's work in their own strength.

- The transformed are participants, while the conformed want to be spectators.
- The transformed have a different set of values that reflects the glory of God, while most conformers are content to attend church, discuss budgets, give their money to larger buildings needed or not and provide entertainment rather than true worship each Sunday.
- The transformed aren't concerned about who gets the credit, so long as the work is correctly completed.
- The transformed are content to live a pleasing life before God and serve others.
- The conformed often follow the latest fads [in all things] with little concern from where they originated or whether they line up with true biblical principles.
- The conformed are satisfied with the status quo and does not welcome a transforming experience of worship because life is more comfortable just as it presently is.

What happens if the church repents and returns to God's program?

Even the mention of returning to true spiritual worship is not popular, because the church that returns would:

- Lose many carnally minded people.
- Suffer drastic cuts in the budget.
- Lose their superstars.
- Lose the dead weight that possesses a twisted set of spiritual values.

Positive change is possible

- To have a new spiritual reality.
- To have people who praise and glorify God and not people.
- To have a new unity among the children of God.
- To also serve one another and reach the world for Christ.

Certainly, all our problems would not be solved and instead we would face a new set of challenges generated by spiritual growth in ministry. The upside is simply the fact that these are Spirit-led endeavors rather than carnally influenced and coerced ideas. As a pastor and theology educator I encounter more and more church leaders who are accepting whatever sad situation [for example: pornography addiction of both men and women, cohabitation, unsaved people helping to lead worship, high school aged children cross dressing in school, and same-sex activity moving openly into the church]. They get their way in the church, because the membership is afraid of offending the world; having bought into such garbage as "political correctness" rather than "biblical correctness." So many Christians are individually and corporately experiencing all of this as a new normal, when it's the same old satanic deceptive strategy, ["what I can't conquer – I will defile!"]

Many of the solutions offered for ministry today are unbiblical and void of the supernatural. More and more of our churches are finding themselves in a religious rut similar I imagine to the old pioneer trails heading west, once you've found one just follow on and stay in the rut to the end. When you get there you will know where you are?

If we look to the church for our model for conduct rather than to the Spirit and the Word, we will find little encouragement to apply the cross of Christ to our covetous idolatries. The Word and the Spirit admonishes us not to be conformed to the world, but the church generally fails to respond. Today many church people look much like their counterparts lost in the world without Christ.

- They think like them in many ways.
- They value so many of the same things of the world.
- They have so many of the world's same practices and habits.

Those who would really be different for Christ's sake are often shunned as intolerant bigots or know-it-alls even within the church. The Apostle Paul gives us a picture of what God would have us to be in the third chapter of Colossians. Prayerfully notice the beginning verses admonishes us to give our attention to the things above where Christ is at the right hand of the Father.

Then he counseled us to put to death our covetous idolatries that bring the wrath of God upon the lost. From there we are urged to put off the old man with his deeds and put on the new man. After the admonition to let the peace of God rule in our hearts, we are told to let the Word of Christ dwell in us richly, teaching and admonishing one another with psalms, hymns, and spiritual songs, doing all in the name of Jesus with thanksgiving. It's obvious if we are to let the word of Christ dwell in us richly, some outright adjustments and changes will have to be made.

Trading preferences

More and more people become addicted to sugars daily. Knowing that this will probably result in their physical poisoning by their passion for sweet things, as this addiction grows for sweets – their taste for healthy foods such as fruits and vegetables begin to disappear.

Just so, Christians who feed their passions for the things of this world lose their desire for heavenly things. It is my prayer that we will stop striving to see just how much of this world we can hold onto and still be an effective Christian. Instead, see how much of the world and its many fancies you can let go out of your life, trading preferences for Christ who is your life. Engaged in activities that fill our minds with the words and works of this world results in putting on the old man and his deeds. May we remain closely intimate with our Lord and Savior and not fall short of our goals. We must filter all things through the truth of God's Word.

Just because a thing has been practiced for a thousand years does not mean it is right. On the other hand, because a thing has not been practiced for a thousand years does not mean it is wrong.

The Spirit of Truth

The Holy Spirit has the assignment of revealing spiritual truth to all believers-priests. He is called the "Spirit of truth" (see John 14:17; 15:26; 16:13). Jesus said the Holy Spirit would, "teach you all things, and bring to your remembrance all the things I said to you" (John 14:26).

"He will guide you into all truth; for He will not speak on His own authority, but whatever He hears He will speak; and He will tell you things to come. He will glorify Me, for He will take of what is Mine and declare it to you" (John 16:13-14).

A thorough study of the three chapters mentioned above [John 14, 15, and 16] will enlighten you that the Holy Spirit is a Person and without Him you or the church can do nothing. It is the plan of God, individually and corporately, the way He sets our encounters with Him. In their book *"Experiencing God,"* Henry T. Blackaby & Claude V. King clarifies this point. Notice:

- When God spoke to Moses and others in the Old Testament, those events were encounters with God.

- An encounter with Jesus was an encounter with God for His disciples.
- In the very same manner, an encounter with the Holy Spirit is an encounter with God for us.[8]

Now that the Holy Spirit is here, He is the One who *guides* you, the true believe-priest, individually and the church corporately into all truth and teaches you all things. Without Him the church or the believer will never get out of that rut of religion! However, with Him:

- You receive *deep* spiritual truth because of the Holy Spirit working in your life.
- You can understand the Word of God and live the deeper life in Christ because the Holy Spirit *reveals* it and teaches you [the truth].
- When coming to the Word of God, the Holy Spirit is always present to instruct you.
- You never discover Spiritual and biblical truth; it is revealed by the Spirit.
- When the Holy Spirit reveals truth to you, He is not leading you to an encounter with God – this is an encounter with God!

When the Holy Spirit speaks to your heart audibly or through His Word what you do next is very crucial. The Scripture warns, if God speaks and you do not respond to Him, a time could come when you will not hear His voice. Disobedience can lead to:

> *"Behold, the days are coming," says the Lord God,*
> *That I will send a famine on the Land,*
> *Not a famine of bread,*
> *Not a thirst for water,*
> *But of hearing the words of the Lord.*
> *They shall wander from sea to sea,*
> *And from north to east.*
> *They shall run to and fro, seeking*
> *the word of the Lord,*
> *But shall not find it.*
> *– Amos 8:11-12*

I repeat, Spiritual truths can only be revealed by God:

> *"Eye has not seen, nor ear heard, nor have entered into the heart of man the things which God has prepared for those who love Him." But God has revealed them to us through His Spirit. For the Spirit searches all things, yes the deep things of God. For what man knows the things of a man which is in him? Even so no one knows the things of God except the Spirit of God. Now we have received, not the spirit of the world, but the Spirit who is from God, that we might know the things that have been freely given us by God"* (1 Corinthians 2:9-12).

Don't fail to make necessary changes in your life from a single word you receive from the Lord. Then God will do in and through you, everything He says to you.

Recent research shows that only 25% of the Christians in America believe in the Holy Spirit. Add to that – many who believes He exists but will not make room for Him to operate His ministries in them individually or corporately. Barna's research has similar results as those Jesus spoke of in Matthew 13 wherein of the four soils three did not produce equal fruits. However, the one that was fruitful produced three types of fruit, some a hundredfold, some sixty-fold, some thirty-fold.

Can you see how the ruts to nowhere are formed? Could we have been wrong so long that we have convinced ourselves that what we are doing is right? I'm sure that any farmer with this difference in soil qualities would probably order an immediate soil analysis.

Word of the kingdom

In Matthew 13:10-11, Jesus entertains a question from His disciples concerning His teaching methods. They asked why He taught in parables. He answered them, "Because it has been given to you to know the mysteries of the kingdom of heaven, but to them it has not been given." Here Matthew alludes to the unbelief of the people being the cause of their spiritual blindness (13:11). Jesus clarifies the message to His disciples and us in (v. 19), "When anyone hears the words of the kingdom, and does not understand it, then the wicked *one* comes and snatches away what was sown in his heart." He further explains how we receive and understand the words of the kingdom due to the condition of our hearts:

1. Some fell by the wayside this heart is hard making it impossible for the seed (word) to penetrate [understand] the ground's surface, which is packed by heavy traffic. Satan easily snatches it away.
2. Some fell on stony ground, this person hears the word and receives it with joy – but he or she has no root within themselves to endure; so when tribulation or persecution come, because of the word, immediately he or she stumbles. This ground (heart) is too shallow for understanding.
3. Some fell among thorns and the thorns sprang up and choked them. He hears the word, and the cares of the world and deceitfulness of riches choke the word and it becomes unfruitful.
4. Some fell on good ground [hearts] these are those who *hear* the Word and *understand it;* and he or she in deed bears fruit [three types of fruit: some a hundredfold, some sixty, some thirty.

There were three different grounds in the parable that produced no fruit and the fourth produced three kinds with fruit. The point here is for various reasons the yields produced are not equal, but all three [hearts] are fruitful; and putting God's glory on display before the world. The Scripture says,

"You will know them by their fruits" (Matthew 7:16)." *"By this My Father is glorified, that you bear much fruit, so you will be My disciples"* (John 15:8).

True believers obey the Lord's commands, submitting to His precious Word. Because of their commitment to God's Word, they are devoted to His will, thus their prayers are fruitful (study carefully John 14:13, 14, 21, 23).

Jesus, the final cure

Christ gave specific prescriptions for the sick church (of the ruts) of the end-times. Parenthesis added for emphasis. He reminded the blind church of Laodicea that they needed more than precious salve to see – they needed the truth of God's Word which only Christ could bring them. Think of those churchgoers today who "enjoy" the sermon and the music and leave without any change of heart!

Jesus' final prescription is a positive cure for their compromise, spiritual poverty, nakedness, and blindness that characterized [Laodicea] the end-time church. The greatest invitation in the Bible:

> ***"Behold I stand at the door and knock: if any man hears My voice, and open the door, I will come into him and will sup with him, and he with Me"*** (Revelation 3:20).

Condition of the church

- When Jesus came the first time He was not received by His own people (see John 1:11).
- When Christ was here, He predicted that His Second Coming would also be met with unbelief (see Luke 18:8).
- The condition of the church when Christ returns is Christlessness, notice He says, *"If anyone hears My voice ...... I will come into him [or her]* (see Revelation 2:20).Emphasis added.
- The hierarchy in many local churches has denied Christ's entrance, because they prefer an organization [flesh] that they can control over an organism [spiritual] which only Christ, the Head can control!
- O how He loves us – He still knocks on the door of each person's heart.
- We must all remember He does not force His way in.
- No one is saved against his or her own will – no one is compelled to love and obey Him who wants to be rebellious!

REFLECTION AND DISCUSSION QUESTIONS: CHAPTER 7

1. We worship Christ and behold His glory as we are transformed by His Spirit into His image. In a few words explain the process below:

2. Discuss how the Spirit transforms us into "living sacrifices" with "renewed minds" reflecting the glory of God.

3. Discuss the effects of the transformed and the conformed in the church.

4. What happens if the church repents and returns to the truth of God's Word?

5. Discuss the importance of the Spirit of truth's ministry in the believer and the church.

6. I can apply this lesson to my life by:

7. Closing Statement of Commitment:

CHAPTER EIGHT

Approaching God in Worship

LORD, who may abide in Your tabernacle?
Who may dwell in Your holy hill?
(Psalm 15:1).

In earlier chapters we witnessed these questions answered in the priests' worship of God in the Tabernacle of Moses. The requirements for approaching God in the holy places meant:

- The worshiper came not without blood.
- The worshipper was clean through the Word.
- The worshipper was free of un-confessed or un-judged sin.
- The worshipper had access through one Spirit.

Psalm 15 leads the reader to the central issues of true worship namely, in the character of those who may properly approach and dwell with the LORD. In this beautiful Psalm, David structured it using a question to answer methodology:

Lord who may abide in Your tabernacle. Who may dwell in Your holy hill?

- *He who walks uprightly* (v. 2).
- *He who does not backbite with his tongue* (v. 3).
- *In whose eyes a vile person is despised* (v. 4).
- *He who does these things shall never be moved* (v. 5).

The questions of the psalm magnify the worshipper's attraction to the presence of God. The tabernacle worship was according to pattern *"lest you die."*

Therefore, coming into the divine presence of God:

- The worshipper was to experience fear, but at the same time attraction.
- The worshipper was to pay attention to detail [according to pattern].
- The worshipper was to put aside all other earthly duties to enter the sanctuary.
- The worshipper was to enjoy covenant relationship with God.
- The worshipper was terrified in the sense of their total dependency to the will of God.
- All worshippers are to stand at the entrance waiting on God. It is His house and He is the host. The privilege to enter must be granted – *the worshippers are His guests!*

Wisdom from Old Testament worship

Psalm 15 passes wisdom on to us for worshippers desiring true worship. The two questions at the beginning of this Psalm give much direction for our consideration concerning true worship:

- The worshipper should be aware of his or her separation from God. Only lost people can be found. Come with the proper attitude.
- The worshipper should realize that he or she must be received into God's presence and by His standards not their own.
- The worshipper should be aware of His presence.
- The worshipper should realize the old saying, "the ground is level at the Cross." Meaning no one stands above the other. Pride, position, nor station in life have place here.
- The worshippers should realize they are all 100% dependent on the Lord.
- God has drawn the worshipper into relationship with Him for this life and for the life to come.
- The worshipper wants to be there.
- The Lord is the worshipper's sure foundation.
- The worshippers' character traits are godly, as evidenced in their ethical-moral standards of living.

God's instructions in the Old Testament regarding all aspects of the tabernacle with which the worship of Israel was identified were given to Moses in specific details. God admonished him on several occasions to take great care that all things were done *"according to pattern"* which God had given him (see Exodus 25:9, 40; 26:30; 27:8; Hebrews 8:5). In verse 34 we see the results of Moses doing exactly as he was commanded, there we read:

> *"Then a cloud covered the tent of the congregation, and the glory of the Lord filled the tabernacle."* It was God's response to a work done strictly according to His Word.

Wisdom from New Testament Worship

The Priesthood of Aaron and the tabernacle, or temple made by human hands with all its elaborate ritual, came to an end after fifteen hundred years at the sacrifice of Christ. By Christ's *one sacrifice,* which He offered *"once and for all,"* we know that the question of sin has been settled before a Holy God for every sinner, who:

- trusts in this finished work of Christ
- receives Him by faith as their own personal Savior
- owns Him as Lord
- is eternally saved

The devil loves to play mind games, and many times through friends or through a doubting brother or sister, he plants a seed of doubt and unbelief in the believer's mind concerning the word "eternal." Thus, he will set up a stumbling block that if not taken care of immediately can stunt your spiritual growth for life. Don't let the devil dumb you down!

Notice, because the problem of sin is settled and by faith the believer has received Christ as personal Savior, he or she is constituted, *a priest unto God,* with the privilege of coming into His presence to worship. Christ is now the believer's great High Priest and through Him, each believer may come *boldly* into the presence of God, and offer to Him the sacrifice of his or her heart's appreciation in praise and worship (carefully study Hebrews 9:10; 13:15; 1 Peter 2:5).

A careful examination of the New Testament reveals the fact that worship is no longer connected with a tabernacle or a temple made by human hands. It is so sad; many Christians and churches miss the truth of this point. As we study the pages of the Books of Acts and the Epistles, we find certain well established characteristics which defined the early church – as *led by the Holy Spirit;* they established assembling together in the name of the Lord Jesus Christ, in church fellowship. Some believe the Holy Spirit came on the Day of Pentecost and the church was born, but then He went back to Heaven afterward, leaving the church and Scripture to man and reason.

God's plan is clearly seen in the New Testament as it was in the Old Testament tabernacle. The church was to be built by the Holy Spirit as was the tabernacle, *"according to pattern;* that pattern begins with the Holy Spirit fulfilling His role as Christ's Chief Operating Officer; working to build His Church of Holy Spirit-filled believer-priests, the body of Christ, of which Christ alone is the Head. The mission of that Church is the expansion of the kingdom of God on the earth through making disciples, teaching them to obey all the things the Lord has commanded.

The kingdom of God is not based on doctrine only; but it is also founded on *relationships* – relationships with God and, because of God, relationships with one another. Scriptural doctrine help define those relationships. Many Christians seem to be "anti-doctrine" because many manmade doctrines have been brought in over time that is made to simply appear as virtues. However, these doctrines are the apostles' doctrine, the God-breathed Scriptures that must be kept pure of manmade contamination.

Perfect Unity

A lawyer asked Jesus which was the greatest commandment. We can gain much truth from His reply,

> *"You shall love the Lord your God with all your heart, and with all your soul, and with all your mind, and with all your strength.' The second is this, You shall love your neighbor as yourself"* (Mark 12:30-31).

Jesus said the second commandment is like the first. When you love God, your love for others will be like your love for God – the second is like the first. The more you unconditionally love God, the more you will unconditionally love others. But you cannot truly have Jesus and at the same time disobey what He says. The point is the kingdom of God is most perfectly revealed in our relationships to one another.

We are one

We are being perfected into a unity (see John17). To be in the kingdom, we must be committed to one another as individuals and as a church:

If Christ accepts us while we are still *imperfect* – we must accept one another.

Many think they are open to God while harboring something in our heart that someone has done to them, if you fail to forgive or fail to overlook a weakness in another – not only will your heart harden toward that person, but also against God. You may not like what they have done, but love is your only choice. The Scriptures are clear, "The one who does not love his brother [or sister] whom he has seen, cannot love God whom he has not seen" (1 John 4:20).

Pentecost and beyond

The Book of Acts is the only book in the New Testament that has no recorded end, which means the Acts of the Apostles continues today, on-going through Holy Spirit-filled disciples "according to pattern." I've mentioned this several times in other chapters of this book, but it bears repeating, God has never left His plan to man's imagination, opinions or dreams.

The Holy Spirit came to be in us and guide us into all truth. So, it should be understood by all in the church, we cannot know Spiritual truth except God reveal it to us – and He does through the Holy Spirit and His Word! Jesus said, "I am the Way, the Truth and the Life."

Church begins in Worship

Many in and out of the church would love to make Christianity just another world religion; and then it would simply require obedience to certain rituals and rules supposedly from founders long dead; and therefore, commitment and accountability are relative. We will explore this point in further detail in a later chapter. Our Founder is very much alive forever more! He is Jesus Christ, the Head of His body, the Church. In the church everything begins with worship and every act is done *"as unto the Lord!"* Remember in the Old Testament everything began with worship and it was done *"lest you die!"* Notice, the command in each, the Old and New Testament is clearly expressing *"according to pattern!"*

Pattern does not include opinions or interpretation

One of the greatest hindrances to true worship is the thought and it is only a thought, that the New Testament Scriptures contain rules and regulations governing an *"order of service"* for the meeting of the saints to worship. No, no, what we find are certain broad *principles* therein, to which we would do well to obey and follow *as a pattern!"* I remember when our three daughters were growing up, I would tag along with my wife as she searched through various stores which carried patterns for dressmaking.

On the outside of the packet was a picture of the result – just the right pattern for making three blouses and skirts or three look-a-like dresses and sometimes one of the same for herself. When she would descend on her cutting table to cutout the pieces then sew them together, she always made it according to the pattern. Any deviation from the picture changed the pattern from the true.

My wife is an industrious Proverb 31 woman. As we moved from one duty station another we always had a sewing room set aside for her sometimes before we could finish unpacking the door bell would ring as some client from our last duty station had no doubt called a friend in the area we were moving into informing them of my wife's skill and ability to follow the pattern – making the dresses according to pattern.

Running through the Book of Acts, the Pauline and the General Epistles is a pattern for true worship individually and corporately. However, our calling to that true pattern of worship comes only through the Holy Spirit and the truth of God's Word working in tandem.

And what a calling it is! In the very first chapter of the Book of Acts the pattern begins to appear. Jesus said,

"You shall receive power after the Holy Spirit has come upon you ...." (Acts 1:8).

This passage of Scripture is not part of a religion, it denotes a life. Worship is our purpose for being – it is our very life in Christ! The *power* in Acts 1:8 was for a new task – God empowered His disciples to be faithful witnesses even when they faced the most fearsome opposition as they took the gospel of the kingdom to the ends of the earth. The New Testament believer-priests are commissioned and empowered to the same task of telling others about Christ regardless of the consequences – the Book of Acts is still being written! The same power of the Holy Spirit that raised Jesus from the tomb empowered the church of the first century to turn the world upside down is working in true believer-priests today! It has been said:

It has been said, "It is far greater to attempt something great and fail – then to just sit down and do nothing."

REFLECTION AND DISCUSSION QUESTIONS: CHAPTER 8

1. List four requirements for Priest's approach to holy place:
    a.
    b.
    c.
    d.

2. Explain the phrase, "according to pattern."

3. Through Christ our _____ _____ every believer can come boldly into the presence of God.

4. We cannot know spiritual truth unless _____ _____ it.

5. The Word of God and the Holy Spirit work in _____.

6. I can apply this lesson to my life by:

7. Closing Statement of Commitment:

CHAPTER NINE

Worship in Spirit

"...... a time is coming and has now come when the true worshippers will worship the Father in spirit and in truth, for they are the kind of worshippers the Father seeks. God is spirit, and His worshippers must worship in spirit and in truth"
(John 4:23-24).

In John 4, Jesus held a conversation with a Samaritan woman; whose inquisitiveness asked Jesus some questions about true worship. From Jesus' revelatory answers we gain much insight concerning true worship. According to the passage we learn that:

- God, the Father in heaven seeks a certain kind of worshipper.
- We worship the Living God who wants us to be a worshipper according to pattern [as defined in the passage].
- The kind of worship God seeks is God-centered, meaningful and transforming to our souls.
- The worship God seeks must be worship in *"spirit"* that springs up from the "spring of living water" within the true believer (see vv. 13-14).
- God is spirit those who worship Him must worship Him in spirit ......"

The human spirit

Our worship must match the very nature of God; therefore, we must thoroughly understand what *"spirit"* is and this will help us to become the worshippers God is seeking.

God Himself is "spirit"– and each of us has a human "spirit."

What is important for us to see here is that the human spirit is the primary concern in true worship because God Himself is "spirit," and true worshippers' worship "in spirit" [their own human spirit]. Jesus told the woman at the well that,

> *"a time is coming*
> *and has come*
> *when the true worshipper*
> *will worship the Father*
> *in spirit and truth"*
> – John 4:23

Jesus was saying the focus is shifting away from the legitimacy of places of worship, which the woman at the well had raised. There was a day coming, in fact, it is already here – when the only real question would be whether true worship *was happening in the spirit of the worshipper.*

Therefore, through our human spirit, quickened [made alive] and enabled by the Holy Spirit in regeneration puts our *soul* back in its rightful place of subjection to the spirit along with the body. God's order is spirit, soul, and body.

Satan's order is body, soul, and spirit, to which we can bear witness through the billions of dollars spent annually on commercials, cosmetics, plastics, gyms and anything else that people think will enhance the looks of their body for another few days, or months, or years.

Unfortunately, the human spirit has been relatively *overlooked* even by Christian theology. As the soul comprising our mind, will, emotions, attitudes, worldviews, personality, conflicts, and all the rest that we are has been the focus.

As a result, assumptions from science and cultural reasoning are running rampart while tossing out absolute moral truth. Taking the lead in this humanistic ploy are public opinion, academia, media, governments, school boards and public-school systems across this nation:

- Science holds that a person is a dichotomy or body and soul, with the spirit a part of the soul.
- Others speak of the body and soul with a blank slate and the spirit as being non-existent.
- Feelings, [a component of the soul] are quickly becoming the number one determining factor in most situations in today's culture.

Also neglected and rejected has been the truth of God's Word. In the Scripture concerning the spirit, soul, and body, the apostle Paul says,

> *"Now may the God of peace Himself sanctify you completely and may your whole spirit, soul, and body be preserved blameless at the coming of our Lord Jesus Christ"* (1Thessalonians 5:23).

> *"For the Word of God is living and powerful, and sharper than any two-edged sword, piercing even to the division of soul and spirit and of joints and marrow, and is a discerner of the thoughts and intents of the heart"* (Hebrews 4:12).

Paul's comprehensive reference to the term "completely" emphasizes here as with the writer of Hebrews that the spirit, soul and body are three different entities.

Figure 3

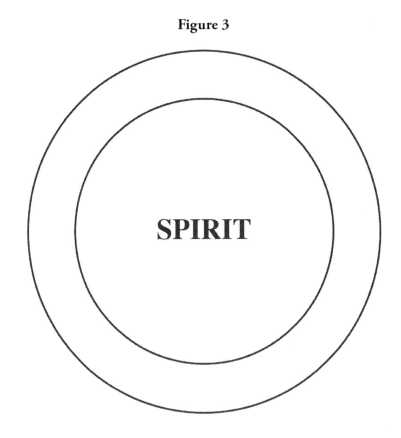

Realizing the spirit and soul are immaterial and the body material, a dichotomy – the Word of God working in tandem with the Spirit of God has the power to make them three realities, a trichotomy. The Scripture says,

"And the Lord God formed man of the dust of the ground and breathed into his nostrils the breath of life; and man became a living soul" (see Genesis 2:7). KJV [Some of the other versions use "living being"].

So, we see that God created man [Adam], the material [body] from the dust of the earth relating him to the earth. He is described as "flesh" – but God breathed into him the breath of life, the immaterial or spiritual [spirit/ soul]. God is spirit and He created man in His image, [spirit]. Adam was God-conscious through his human spirit for worship and fellowship – that is until sin came and he became self-conscious and opened the door of his soul – at the same time closing the door of his spirit to God:

- Sin closed the door to a day to day fellowship with God for Adam and Eve as it alienated them from Him.
- Alienation from God meant Adam's spirit died for the light of God had gone out.
- Adam now has a conscious meaning he knew right from wrong, which gave him the ability to make choices.
- Being spiritually dead, the door was open for his soul which comprises his mind, will and affections [feelings] to control his being.
- This new soul-man Adam now has a sin nature and has become self-reliant and estranged from God.

Having chosen the tree of the knowledge of good and evil over the tree of life – put him in league with the devil. God *mercifully* put Adam and Eve out of the Garden of Eden where Adam had forfeited his God given-dominion over creation to Satan (see Genesis 1:26-27).

Humanity's predicament meant alienation and separation from God to the point of hopelessness. There was no human way for them to reach God because of the sin nature within them. Man is depraved, (prayerfully study Genesis 2-3). And please notice how God goes to work immediately to rescue fallen humanity – God promised He would provide a way out for them [a Redeemer]:

> *"And I will put enmity*
> *Between you and the woman,*
> *And between your seed and her*
> *He shall bruise your head,*
> *And you shall bruise His heel"*
> Genesis 3:15

This "first gospel" is prophetic of the struggle and its outcome between "your seed" [Satan and unbelievers, who are called the devil's children in John 8:44) and her Seed [Christ, a descendent of Eve and those in Him], which began in the Garden of Eden in the midst of the curse passage – a message of hope came forth – the woman's offspring called *"He"* is Christ, who will one day defeat the Serpent.

Paul in a passage very similar to Genesis 3 encouraged the believers in Rome saying, "And the God of peace will crush Satan shortly" (Romans 16:20). Praise God we [believers] are going to participate in the crushing of Satan for we are the woman's seed through our Savior and His finished work on the cross. Because of Christ's finished work on the cross – the Holy Spirit can bring salvation to every person desiring it!

The early churches, which began as a result of God's blessing on the preaching of the apostles and others *multiplied* in an astounding manner as recorded in the book of Acts of the Apostles. Later letters, as mentioned earlier were written by Divine inspiration addressed to various churches and assemblies.

These letters were written to correct certain errors and abuses, for example, Paul's letters to the Corinthians and the Galatians. Others wrote concerning the establishment of doctrine, and encouragement. Herein we have all the guidance needed for worship in spirit and in truth for the people of God.

REFELECTION AND DISCUSSION QUESTIONS: CHAPTER 9

1. God, the Father _____ a certain kind of worshipper.

2. Discuss the kind of worship God seeks is _____ _____.

3. In Genesis __: _____, God promised a way out for man [a Redeemer].

4. The purpose of Paul's letters was to correct certain _____ and _____.

5. Others wrote concerning the establishment of _____ and _____.

6. I can apply this lesson to my life by:

7. Closing Statement of Commitment:

CHAPTER TEN

Worship in Truth

"....a time is coming and has now come when the true
worshippers will worship the Father in spirit and truth, for
they are the kind of worshippers the Father seeks. God is spirit,
and His worshippers must worship in spirit and in truth"
(John 4:23-24).

In chapter nine we examined worship in spirit, as Jesus and the woman at the well continue to converse in John 4 another issue emerges. The woman admits her questionable past and Jesus responds, "What you have said is true" (see John 4:16-18). Later this proves to be a turning point for the woman (v. 39). She surmised that if Jesus knew things about her that was humanly impossible to know, she was convinced that He knew the *truth* about many other things.

The woman then turns to a subject that caused major contention between the Jews and Samaritans, the right place of worship. Jesus takes advantage of the opportunity in this teachable moment to move beyond her current conception to what matters most.

Compared to that, the place of worship proves rather insignificant, especially when considering "a time is coming *and now has come* when the true worshippers will neither worship the Father on this mountain nor in Jerusalem (v. 21). Jesus presses on, "not only is this kind of worship coming, but it has already come." The woman asserts, "I know that Messiah [Christ] is coming. When He comes, He will explain everything to us" (v. 25). Jesus proclaimed to her, *"I who speaks to you am He"* (v.26). This *truth* is larger than anything this woman could imagine at the beginning of the conversation. But she became convinced and so did many other Samaritans. Later in verse (v. 42b) the Samaritans exclaimed, "We know that this is *truly* the Savior of the world."

No particular place

The point is clear, salvation is of the Jews – but to worship the Savior does not require any particular place of worship, so the Samaritans are no longer required to go to Jerusalem to worship. What it does require is that *truth* wells up from within the worshipper's human spirit – through the that regenerating and transforming work of the Holy Spirit (see chapter 9). So, the type of worship the Father seeks contains truth along with spirit.

Ultimately, the truth that Jesus is speaking of here is about Himself *as the Word of God incarnate* – *"the Truth:"* Jesus said, "I am the way and the *truth* and the life; no one comes to the Father except through me" (see John 14:6). So, worship that is acceptable to the Father (John 4:21-24) begins with *accepting Jesus as the Messiah [Savior]*.

If we are going to worship God, the Father – we must accept His expression of "truth" in His Son!

Truth in action

One of the names given of the Holy Spirit in John's gospel is the "Spirit of truth" (study carefully John 14:17; 15:26). Jesus promised, "When He the Spirit of *truth*, comes He will guide you into all truth" (16:13). So, for John spirit and truth eventually comes together in the worshipper when he or she worships the Father acceptably [in spirit and in truth].

In the encounter in John 4, *Truth* begins with biblical truth about the place of worship and ends up with Spiritual truth about the very nature of God (God is spirit) and the incarnate presence of the Son of God (Jesus the "Messiah").

Yes, Jesus is the truth, and those who worship the Father must not only believe He is the truth – but we must live according to the standards of the truth manifest in Him by weaving Christ and the truth He proclaims into all aspects of our lives.

Truth in true worship

To worship "in spirit and truth" is living the kind of life to the Father that brings the work of the Holy Spirit and the human spirit into unity.

Thus, the impact of the *truth* embodied and made manifest in the Son is the practice of God's presence in the whole of life as clearly seen in the following scriptural example:

Present your body

The apostle Paul in the role of a counselor encourages his readers,

"I beseech you therefore, brethren, by the mercies of God, that you present your bodies a living sacrifice, Holy, acceptable to God, which is your reasonable service" (Romans 12:1).

In Romans 12:1 Paul turns the corner as if saying, in chapters 1-11 I gave you a foundation of doctrinal truth, follow it by applying it to your "whole person" throughout your lives. Doctrine precedes the exhortations and furnishes the basics for a Christian walk. Live the truth!

Before a person can live right, he or she must think right about God, Christ, the blood, the Spirit and the Word; and if a person does not need sound doctrine, he or she cannot produce true Christian living. Truth! A real born-again experience, by grace through faith in the shed blood of Jesus – precedes a holy life, and apart from the new birth true holy living is totally impossible for any human being.

A living sacrifice

This "living sacrifice" is in glorious contrast to the dead "legal sacrifices." The death of the one "Lamb of God which takes away the sins of the world" (John 1:29) has swept all dead sacrifices from the altar of God, to make room for the *redeemed themselves* as "living sacrifices" to God who "made Him (Christ) to be sin for us" (II Corinthians 5:21).

Every outreach of a Christian's heart
in grateful praise and
every act prompted
by the love of Christ,
is itself
A sacrifice to God
of sweet-smelling savor.
– (Hebrews 13:15, 16 NCV)

As the Old Testament sacrifices offered without *blemish* to God were regarded as holy, so are New Testament believer-priests, who yield themselves to God holy.

> *"As those that are alive from the dead, and their members as instruments of righteousness unto God"* (Romans 6:13) are, in God's eyes, not ritually but in reality, "holy and acceptable unto Him."

When we have done those things, which are acceptable unto God, we should face the spiritual fact that what we have done is our *"reasonable service!"*

The Scripture goes on to exhort the Roman Christians and us to live as sacrifices; by recalling God's mercies toward us hell-deserving sinners and take immediate action of "presenting our bodies" which is the only proper response of those who are the recipients of that mercy. Paul uses bodies, a comprehensive term for the whole person without attempting to differentiate the parts – spirit, soul and body (see 1 Thessalonians 5:23; also see Hebrews 4:12).

A heart for God

When the person obediently and sacrificially has a *heart* for God – God will honor that person. As the renewed soul willingly follows the born-again spirit so will the body follows the renewed soul. This agreement is God's order and His will. This indicates a heart for God as in the examples of Abel, Abraham, Moses and many New Testament saints; however, our best example is Jesus Himself. As a Man, He demonstrated the highest humility [faithfulness, obedience and totally yielded will] toward His Father [1 unity] see figure 4 below:

Figure 4

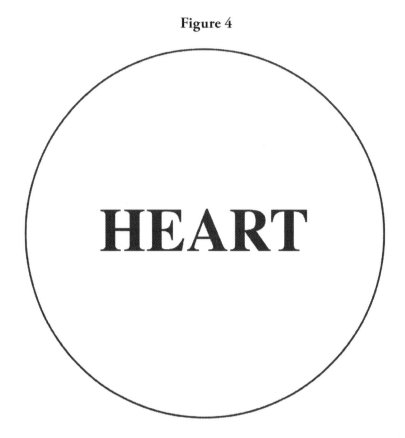

All of us belong to God, so the only sensible thing to do is live the life of a "holy and pleasing" sacrifice to God. Since Jesus came to become a sacrifice in our stead:

> *"For even the Son of Man did not come to be served, but to serve, and to give His life a ransom for many"* (Mark 10:45).

> *"And being found in appearance as a man, He humbled Himself and became obedient to the point of death, even the death of the cross"* (Philippians 2:8).

After the humbling of *incarnation*, Jesus further humbled Himself in that He did not demand normal human rights but subjected Himself to suffering and persecution at the hands of unbelievers. The only way we can become like Christ is if we give ourselves as sacrifices. "Truly, this is worship in truth!"

REFLECTION AND DISCUSSION QUESTIONS: CHAPTER 10

1. What was the woman's explanation of Christ's knowledge of her?

2. Salvation is of the _____.

3. Discuss the importance of truth in worship:

4. Paul exhorts his readers to live as sacrifices. What was his purpose here?

5. Discuss what it means to give ourselves as living sacrifices, in contrast to legal sacrifices.

6. I can apply this lesson to my life by:

7. Closing Statement of Commitment:

SECTION V

Farther Along

CHAPTER ELEVEN

Do not be Conformed

*"And do not be **conformed** to this world, but be transformed by the renewing of your mind, that you many prove what is that good and acceptable and perfect will of God"*
(Romans 12:2).

Do not be conformed to this world. This is neither a recommendation nor a suggestion, but a command! Conformed *(summorphizo GK)* means to make of like form with another person or thing.[9] The believer does not conform when he or she assumes an outward expression that does not come from within, nor is it representative of his or her inner life.

The same Greek word for "conform" is translated "fashion" in 1 Peter 1:14: "…. not fashioning yourselves according to …." In other words, we are not to fashion our lives after this present evil world [age]. Don't let the world form you in its mold:

- This world or age refers to their present secular and atheistic beliefs, values, moral relativism, and multiculturalism – at *any time* current in the world. Jesus referred to the world as humankind's old unregenerate nature.
- The sum of contemporary thinking and values shapes the moral atmosphere of the present world and is always dominated by Satan, the prince of this world's systems (see 2 Corinthians 4:4).
- To be conformed to this age is to yield to the spirit of the present age – that is to follow the path of least resistance until we become like the age to which we conform. Secularism and atheism are on the rise as man seeks to be the end of all things [with no God].

Go with the flow

Today in America, it is expected of you to go with the flow of popular opinion – in this case our relativistic culture of narcissism, multiculturalism, consumerism and materialism. "We the people" has been sent to the fringes through the wishes of media, academia and special interests' groups. As I stated in my book, *Narrow is the Way,*[10] many Christian communities were hit broadside as it came to light that our scientists, lawyers, judges, and politicians are inventing new terminology and language in the courts to get around the absolute moral Law of God; even misinterpreting the Constitution of the United States. Think about it:

- The Holy Bible has been outlawed on public school campuses.
- Biblical truth is now classified as hate speech.
- The truthful Christian is considered prejudice, bigoted and intolerant.
- To witness the gospel to others is considered making others accept our beliefs.
- "We the people" sets absolutely no precedence with our secular politics today.

In his book, *Change to Chains,* William J. Federer states, the Constitution was written to separate power into the executive, legislative, and judicial branches, but since that time other "branches" of power have emerged, such as unions, judges, trial lawyers, environmental groups, financial institutions, and perhaps the most significant, education and media. In America:

The country is controlled by laws.
Laws are controlled by politicians.
Politicians are controlled by voters.
Voters are controlled public opinion.
Public opinion is controlled by media, (Networks,
Hollywood, Internet etc.) and education.
So, whoever controls media and
Education – controls the
Country.[11]

Will Jesus find faith?

Have you given much thought to what the world will be like when the Lord returns? According to the Scripture people will go about the world daily, not fearing God, marrying and eating and drinking and having fun; then Christ will come "as a thief in the night," and they will not be prepared to meet Him. In Noah's day, there was a great deal of *violence* (see Genesis 6:11, 13); and in Lot's time, men gave themselves over to *unnatural lusts* (see Genesis 19:4-11; Romans 1:21). Both characterize America today. The World today is like the days of Noah and Lot, "business as usual" with dwindling fear for the warnings God sends.

When the late Dr. Adrian Rogers was asked if he thought God had turned His back on America he answered, "No America has turned its back on God!"

The failure of the church to participate in the conversation and the shaping of public policy has limited our ability to openly evangelize the lost. We must encourage all the people of God to stand in defense of the Cross of Christ with their spiritual and biblical worldview intact.

No conforming allowed

In the context of making remarks on teaching the Old Testament law in the church, Paul wrote in 1 Timothy 1:5, "Now the purpose of the commandment is *love* from a pure heart, from a good conscience, and from sincere faith, from which some, having strayed have turned aside to idle talk."

Peter uses the Levitical holiness standard, *"Be holy for I am holy,"* (see 1 Peter 1:16) taken from (Leviticus 11:44-45; 19:2) to exhort us to "be not conformed" to the evil desires you had when you lived in spiritual darkness and biblical ignorance. "But just as He who called you is holy, *so be holy in all you do"* (1 Peter 1:14-15).

All the church needs to come into full realization that the Lord meant business in issuing this command! The outcome of our obedience or disobedience to His command will reflect highly in our life-time achievement rewards at the Judgment Seat of Christ.

We are performance oriented by nature and our secularist, materialistic, mechanistic and hedonistic culture enforces that orientation. We want to somehow impress or convince God based on our self-perceived performance. If we've been good as we see it, we feel reasonably safe in our relationship with God.

By the same token, if we have had a horrible day, spiritually we tend to feel insecure, and begin to rationalize, which stunts our spiritual growth as we fail to see the need to grow. To counter this, we still need the gospel everyday to help move away from performance [or works] to a relationship with God based on:

- The sinless life, sin-bearing death and power giving resurrection of Jesus Christ.
- Here we see ourselves from God's perspective, our relationship with Him is not based on our good or bad conduct – but based upon the perfect goodness, death, resurrection and ascension of our Lord and Savior, Jesus Christ.
- Thus, the gospel frees us up to honestly face our sin – knowing that it is now under the blood of Jesus and God is not mad with us nor counting that sin against us (carefully study Romans 4:7-8).
- Daily the gospel reminds the believer that he or she is *in Christ,* as seen by God redeemed, regenerated, justified, sanctified, and blessed with all spiritual blessings in the heavenlies.
- The believer-priest basks in the sunshine of Divine favor; his or her heart goes out in adoration to the One who made it all so blessedly and gloriously real in their *experience.*

We must make it clear, only the regenerated believer can spiritually and intelligently experience the Father and the Son through the power of the indwelling Holy Spirit which is the normal Christian life.

An unsaved person [natural man] though able to recognize God as supreme, and Creator of the universe has not been brought into living relationship with Him as Father and consequently is unable to really appreciate what only the Holy Spirit can reveal. Paul made this clear:

"But the natural man does not receive the things of the Spirit of God, for they are foolishness to him; nor can he know them, because, they are spiritually discerned" (1 Corinthians 2:14).

"But he who is spiritual judges all things, yet he himself is rightly judged by no one" (1 Corinthians 2:14-15).

The natural man [the unconverted], lacks supernatural life and wisdom. Through illumination of the Word, the Holy Spirit provides His saints the capacity to discern truth (see Psalm 119:18). Remember the spiritually dead are unable to comprehend (see John 5:37, 39).Though believer-priests receive illumination from the Spirit, this does not mean:

- That we know everything (Deuteronomy 29:29)
- That we do not need a teacher ((Ephesians 4:11, 12).
- That understanding does not require hard work (2 Timothy 2:15).

The cause of problems in the early churches were more than external worldliness, it was also internal carnality. We suffer a similar problem in churches across America today. An appropriate biblical worldview in the churches is being replaced very subtly with a secular worldview as more and more Christians fail to study their Bibles and make life applications. The present generation is presenting evolution as truth at every level of leadership today even in some churches.

Though this secular theory is making headway in the world – we must stand firm on the absolute truth of the Word. Despite all that has been said to refute these truths, just know, our final exam for our eternal home will be determined from the truths of God's Word! We have an opportunity within our lifetime to study it, apply it and obediently get it right!

REFLECTION AND DISCUSSION QUESTIONS: CHAPTER 11

1. Paul warned that we are not to let the world _____ us.

2. Discuss the three branches of our national government and how is the system of checks and balances operates today?

3. What did Jesus say the world would be like when He returns? Explain.

4. Has the American church succumbed to the performance over grace theology?

5. Discuss how secularism has affected the church, school and family? Explain.

6. I can apply this lesson to my life by:

7. Closing Statement of Commitment:

CHAPTER TWELVE

Truths that Transform

"We all with unveiled face, beholding the glory of the Lord, are being transformed into the same image from one degree of glory to another. "This comes from the LORD who is the Spirit"
(2 Corinthians 3:18).

The biblical change through transformation is hardly mentioned in many churches today. Just as we are commanded not to be conformed to the world; the same passage commands that we be transformed. However, more and more churches are settling for a change in conduct and an improved human morality.

Transformation commanded in the Scripture is a work of the Holy Spirit conducted in the very core of our being. The word *transformed* is used only twice in Scripture:

- We are to be transformed (see Romans 12:2).
- We are being transformed (see 2 Corinthians 3:18).

Both times it is used in the passive voice. Clearly the Holy Spirit is the agent of change in transformation and we are the objects to be changed. This does not mean that we have nothing to do but set back and rely on the Holy Spirit for everything. We do have an active responsibility in transformation. We are to respond through faithful obedience to all moral exhortations and commands in the New Testament. Performance driven [works] and well-intentioned behavior to please God in our own strength – only makes a mess of things in the church and that is unacceptable to God:

- So, just as we must look to Christ rather than our own performance for the assurance and acceptance by a holy God, so we must look to the Holy Spirit to work in us and enable us to do our work.

- Many people are reluctant and hesitant to fully engage with the Holy Spirit because of much erroneous teaching about Him, which causes rejection and neglect of His work in us to our loss.

It is crucial that we are ever mindful of His residency in us, for our bodies are the temple of the Holy Spirit (see 1 Corinthians 6:19). Not only that, Christ Himself dwells within us through the Holy Spirit (see Ephesians 3:16-17); in Christ "the fullness of the Godhead dwells bodily" (see Colossians 2:9). Christ is the vine and we are the branches; all that God has purposed for us is in Christ Jesus (see John 15:5). But it is the Holy Spirit's role to apply the life and power of Christ to us.

He wrote the Book

To fully engage with the Holy Spirit, we should first realize that He is the author of Scripture. Paul wrote, "All Scripture is God-breathed" (2 Timothy 3:16). But God did it through the Holy Spirit. As Peter wrote, "Men spoke from God as they were carried along by the Holy Spirit" (2 Peter 1:21). In the next chapter we will see how important the Scripture is to transformation. The Spirit and the Scripture work in tandem. The Scripture is the primary instrument of the Holy Spirit as He works to transform us. Keep in mind:

- The Holy Spirit quickened us to spiritual life (look again at figure 2)
- The Holy Spirit gave us the Scriptures.
- The Holy Spirit enables us to understand the Scriptures.
- The Holy Spirit directs our path and enables us to apply the Scriptures to our daily lives.
- The Holy Spirit wraps us in the righteousness of Christ.

This work of transformation reminds me of a story I read about a young man, who while taking a walk in the park observed a cocoon attached to a tree limb. As he moved in for a closer look, he noticed a butterfly partially trapped struggling to free itself of the cocoon. On impulse he moved to help the butterfly, at the same time a shout came from a lady behind him, "Don't touch it!" It was too late; the young man had ripped the cocoon open with a stick. The butterfly fluttered to the ground and died.

The young man stood there bewildered. The lady explained to him that he had interrupted a natural process and therefore prevented the butterfly's survival. The struggle being experienced by the butterfly was part of the process of metamorphosis wherein it was being transformed from a caterpillar to a butterfly. As the butterfly struggled for freedom its newly formed wings were being strengthened and conditioned for the last step in the process – of a complete change [transformation] from a caterpillar which naturally crawled around on the ground to a beautiful butterfly in flight.

Sadly many churches like the young man in the illustration have taken a stick called [a discipleship program] and poking around through non-spiritual rote-learning have stunted the spiritual growth of many Christians blocking any real chance of *spiritual and physical deliverance* from access psychological baggage from childhood and other life struggles [never addressed in many churches] and eventual spiritual maturity.

Most of these programs are not holistically oriented and just scratch the surface; never reaching the deep areas of the heart [whole being] of the individual, a work that can only be accomplished by the Holy Spirit through the work of transformation. Notice in 2 Corinthians 5:17 the Scripture says,

> *"Therefore, if anyone is in Christ, he [or she] is a new creation; old things have passed away; behold all things have become new."*

In the brief phrase "in Christ" is the inexhaustible truth of the believer's redemption, which includes the following:

- The believer's security is in Christ, who bore in His body God's full judgment against sin.
- The believer's acceptance is in Him with whom God alone is well pleased.
- The believer's future assurance is in Him who is the resurrection and the life and guarantor of his or her inheritance in heaven.
- The believer shares in the divine nature of Christ, the everlasting Word (see 2 Peter 1:4).

Yes, like the butterfly in the illustration above, we are a new creation which signifies a qualitatively new level of excellence. The New creation refers to regeneration or the new birth (see John 3:3; Ephesians 2:1-3; Titus 3:5). Old things have passed away; priorities, values, beliefs, loves, and plans are gone. The believer has a new perspective on life especially concerning present sin and evil.

The new perspective also includes spiritual growth [*teaching them to obey all that I commanded*] to maturity (a disciple) and service. The genuine new believers have an all-out desire to live righteously, based on the forgiveness of their sins paid for in Christ's substitutionary death (Carefully study Galatians 6:15; Ephesians 4:24). Here many churches drop the ball having no strategy to insure the new believer's spiritual growth.

In his wonderful book, *Mobilizing Men for a One-on- One Ministry,* Steve Sanderman offers a simple biblically based spiritual growth plan that should be considered through its four stages:

1. The 1st stage is the baby Christians and the cry of their hearts is *"feed me."* Their primary *need* is information about the new life in Christ and someone to lovingly care for them and explain these truths and help them along (see 1 Peter 2:2; 1 Corinthians 3:1-3).
2. The 2nd stage is the child Christians, and their cry is *"teach me."* Their primary *need* is the basic truths of the Bible and someone with unconditional love to explain them (see 1 Corinthians 13:11).
3. The 3rd stage is the adolescent Christians, and their cry is *"show me."* Their primary *need* is to find victory over sin and develop a life of obedience to Christ. We need to encourage them to step out on faith. The biblical example Sanderman offers is Paul and Timothy.
4. The 4th and final stage is the adult Christians, and their cry is *"follow me."* Their primary *need* is to use their spiritual gifts in ministry and begin training others. We become co-laborers in the cause of Christ (see 2 Corinthians 8:23; Philippians 2:25; 2 Timothy 2:2).[12]

It's obvious from this assessment that Christians in the various age groups are at different levels in their spiritual growth. Barna research shows that only three out of ten Christians even have a spiritual growth plan. Very few people in our churches have been properly discipled; and the problem caused is obvious by the way church members are living.

History shows that "disciples" were not new when Jesus called His twelve. The word was commonly used among teachers and philosophers of the time:

- To be a disciple – a person must be saved.
- To be a disciple – a person must be delivered.
- To be a disciple – a person must first be a follower.
- To be a disciple – a person has to leave the former way of life.
- To be a disciple – a follower must imitate the one he or she is following.
- To be a disciple – one must be a learner.
- To be a disciple – one must be a reproducer.

When speaking to Timothy, Paul revealed the same vision in 2 Timothy 2:2 where he says,

"And the things you have heard from me among many witnesses, commit these to faithful men who will be able to teach others also."

Here Paul is involving four generations of people. It began when he invited Timothy to join him in Acts 16. As they went about ministering Paul instructed Timothy in the basics of Christianity. He now tells Timothy that the things he has seen and heard in his life he is to pass on to others, who in turn will pass them on to other faithful men [and women]. Bracket is mine.

This is the ministry of multiplication that was seen and taught by Jesus Himself and now modeled and taught by Paul. God's plan is multiplication not addition. I recall reading some time ago of a wall display in the Museum of Natural Science in Chicago, a checkerboard with 64 squares, and in the lower left-hand corner of the board a grain of wheat has been placed.

The display includes the question: "If you doubled the amount of wheat as you move from square to square, how much would you have when you reached the sixty-fourth square?

- A carload?
- A trainload?

The answer, you would have enough wheat to cover the country of India six feet deep." "Are you catching God's vision for our evangelism effort?"

Why are we here [our present location]?

The late Chuck Colson is credited with saying, "The church in America is three thousand miles wide and one inch deep." From Colson's assessment we can readily see why many believers and local churches are where they presently stand.

In answering the title question above, I would ask a question "Does the moon shine?" Certainly, the correct answer would be no as the moon has no light of its own. What we see in the sky night after night is the moon reflecting the light of the sun; we call it [moon light]. Christians are here to reflect the light of the Son individually and corporately to a dying world; the Bible calls it [Christlikeness].

REFLECTION AND DISCUSSION QUESTIONS: CHAPTER 12

1. Transformation happens at the very _____ of our _____.

2. The Holy Spirit is the _____ in transformation however our part is faithful _____ to all moral exhortations and _____ in the New Testament.

3. The _____ _____ gave us the Scriptures.

4. List the cries of the Christian in Saderman's biblically-based spiritual growth plan.

5. Briefly explain the ministry of multiplication in evangelism.

6. I can apply this lesson to my life by:

7. Closing Statement of Commitment:

CHAPTER THIRTEEN

Be Renewed in your Mind

"........ But be transformed by the renewing of your mind ...."
(Rom. 12:2).

In the last two chapters we reviewed two very clear commands the Spirit has recorded in the Scriptures for all Christians in all ages:

- The Christian is not to be conformed or molded by the values of this world.
- They are to be transformed that is completely changed to something else. Transformation takes place only through the renewing of the mind. The result being we have the *"mind of Christ"* (see Philippians 2:5-8).

Spiritual transformation starts in the mind and heart. A mind dedicated to the world and its concerns will produce a life tossed back and forth by the currents of culture. But a mind dedicated to God's truth [a renewed mind] will produce a life that can stand the test of time. We can resist the temptations of our culture by meditating on God's truth and letting the Holy Spirit have free rein in guiding and shaping our thoughts and behaviors. However, to think in any possible way this can be accomplished in your own strength is futile.

The Greek word for "transform" means "to change form," and used to describe an inward renewal of our mind through which our inner spirit is changed to Christlikeness:

- Our regeneration is instantaneous as the Holy Spirit quickens [make alive] our spiritually dead spirit.
- James identifies our transformation as the faith that produces works (see James 2:14-25).

- We are cleansed to Christlikeness in the process of sanctification as we walk in newness of life and spend time in intimate relationship with Him (see 2 Corinthians 3:18).

The battle is raging between your ears

When opposing forces battle within the mind, you must remember that whoever or whatever wins controls your mind and therefore controls you. Thus, when the believer begins to battle between the lusts of the flesh and the will of God, it must be understood that satanic forces are trying to control your being [spirit, soul and body] through your flesh [physical five senses].

I'm sure you see Satan's age-old strategy here, which is simply to get the believer to place their desires before or above God and His will. Remember anything that we put above God and His will is idolatry. Each of us can evaluate whether we are harboring an idol [god]. We are admonished in Matthew 6:33 to "seek first the kingdom of God and His righteousness, and all these things shall be added to you." That is we are to desire God's righteousness and His rule above all that is of the earth (see Matthew 6:9-10).

If you are a true believer, you are now "in Christ," and the Holy Spirit has transformed you and whatever situation you may now be facing, search the Scriptures. I stressed in prior chapters, the Spirit and the Word of God work in tandem. Remember, God brought this piece of spiritual armor out of the spiritual realm into our physical hands for this purpose. It is imperative that we get to know and act upon the principles and the promises of God as found only in the Scriptures.

Living in the Spirit

In Galatians 5:16-18 Paul admonishes all believers, *"So I say, live [walk] by the Spirit [within you], and you will not fulfill the lust of the flesh. For the flesh lusts against the Spirit and the Spirit against the flesh; and these are contrary to one another, so that you do not the things that you wish. But if you are led by the Spirit, you are not under the law."*

The potential of the flesh energized by Satan in the life of the Christian should not be underestimated. Given a chance the flesh will direct our choices. This inner conflict between the flesh and the Spirit is very real. Our local churches are loaded with believers today who carry around about as much mental access baggage as unbelievers;

mainly because the Holy Spirit's ministry of deliverance is not taught and exercised as in the early church. Some individual Christians andchurches are divorcing themselves from the Holy Spirit these days; and therefore, have fallen into human secularism, and reverted to legalism [where man not God is the measure of all things]. These are those who view this conflict as simply the physical flesh and its natural tendencies. Seemingly as the number of Spirit-filled saints decrease; there is an influx of individualistic, self-centered, proud and narcissistic people of the outside culture penetrating the churches across America. This is due mainly to:

- death of the biblical worldview in America
- increased spiritual and biblical illiteracy
- technological advances,
- acute narcissism,
- postmodernism,
- multiculturalism
- a secular humanistic culture
- consumerism and materialism

The reason for the increase in biblical and spiritual illiteracy is in part due to the rejection of truth as many Christian communities are accommodating or striving to blend with this progressive secularism – every Christian community should embrace and teach all members a true biblical worldview. God is real!

I believe Paul was attempting to encourage his people when he wrote, "There is therefore now *no condemnation* to those who are in Christ Jesus, *who do not walk according to the flesh, but according to the Spirit.* For the law of the Spirit of life in Christ Jesus has made me free from the law of sin and death. *"For what the law could not do in that it was weak through the flesh,* **God did by sending His Son in the likeness of sinful flesh, on account of sin: He condemned sin in the flesh – that the <u>righteous requirement</u> of the law might be fulfilled <u>in us who do not walk according to the flesh but according to the Spirit</u>"** (see Romans 8:1- 5). Emphasis added.

I've noticed how people in the public eye are held to the standards of popular opinion guilty or not. However, public opinion can be wrong and, in many cases, – it is wrong; especially when it comes to God, Christ, and the things of God.

Public opinion would think that living in the flesh is the proper way to live; which promotes such philosophies and clichés as, "when trouble comes do the best you can" "God understands," and "with that anything is permissible" "situation ethics" automatically engages as a norm even in many local churches especially such questions in Bible studies as "What's your take on this?" The point is we don't need a point of view; we need the truth of God's Word.

A better understanding of this would be, "Do not be deceived, God is not mocked; whatever a man sows, that he will also reap. For he who sows to his [or her] flesh will of the flesh reap corruption, but he who sows to the Spirit will of the Spirit reap everlasting life" (Galatians 6:7, 8). Emphasis added throughout.

The principle of sowing and reaping was known to everyone in a largely farming society. It is a weak attempt to "mock" God when a Christian thinks that if he or she sows to the *flesh,* they can escape the harvest of destruction and judgment that comes upon those who participate in such accompanying sinful conduct and behavior (see Galatians 5:19-21; Hosea 8:7).

Paul often used the word "flesh" referring to the entire fallen human being; not just the sinful body but the entire being, including the soul and spirit as affected by sin. Then Paul often pitted the "flesh" against the "Spirit" as being two diametrically opposed forces.

The unbeliever can live only in the flesh, but the believer can live in the flesh or in the Spirit – but not at the same time

---

Walking in the Spirit

In contrast with the preceding clear description of sinfulness, Paul depicts the freedom of living in the Spirit. We are no longer under the sentence of the law – but empowered by the Spirit within us to live for Christ. The believer gains the righteous standard of the law – love (see Romans 13:8-10) but not by means of the Law. But we are in Christ and walking in the Spirit, which means we are to order our manner of life and behavior in conformity with the Holy Spirit.

The Law can hold up the standard of righteousness, but it *cannot empower* us to fulfill that standard. Only the Spirit of God can do that. However, the *responsibility* to walk is ours! Notice Daniel for example, when confronted with being defiled through eating the king's food, determined within himself that he would *not give in* to such practice.

Daniel had to make that decision for himself; likewise, we must do the same. No one else could do that for him.

This is the responsibility we too, must meet. Paul's thesis is that everlasting life is the glorious end for those who govern their lives by the inward unction and power of the Holy Spirit; so that He takes over the responsibility to see that we do not fulfill the lusts of the flesh. The new relationship with God results in a new person, who makes a new kind of fruit possible – righteousness! Believer-priests are God's children freed from sin so that we can be given eternal life as a gift by God (see John 3:16).

A renewed mind

Everything you will need from God was placed in you when you were born again. So, the rest of your life is not to try to receive more from God, but rather to renew your mind so you can begin thinking *from the victory* already provided to appropriate it. Then you believe, operate in faith, and release the life of God inside you to the world.

Renewing the mind is like deleting old files from a computer – completely erasing their presence and in their place, loading new files that come as a result of intense love for Christ and deep study of His Word as the Holy Spirit reprograms our minds. Paul is saying, "Allow the truth of God's Word working in tandem with the Spirit to transform you by separating your human spirit from the entanglements of your soul which is brought under the knife work of the Word, bringing the *ruling position over the soul and body* opening your mind to the revealed truth and wisdom by the Spirit.

We must become disciples [learners] of the truth. You cannot be transformed unless you are informed. We can resist the temptations of our culture by meditating day and night on God's truth and as stated earlier, letting the Holy Spirit guide and shape our thoughts and behavior (see Romans 6:22).

You will be transformed by the renewing of your mind. Spiritual transformation begins in the human spirit and mind. The mind is a powerful instrument of the Holy Spirit used to channel kingdom work on earth. A mind dedicated to God's truth through the Spirit of truth will produce a life of truth; that will stand the test of time consistently bringing kingdom truth and reality to earth (see John 16:7-15).

In order to be of proper use to the kingdom, we must be transformed. As we saw earlier, transformed means "changed to another" "changed from within" *GK "Metamorphosis."* In other words, the change on the outside is the natural expression of the nature on the inside.

The caterpillar emerged from the cocoon no longer a caterpillar but changed [transformed] into a beautiful butterfly; there is no such thing as *reverse*-metamorphosis; I believe the same thing holds for true transformation:

- Transformation is fixed with convictions, beliefs and spiritual truths.
- Transformation is not sanctification.
- A transformed [renewed] mind then is other-worldly.
- Our thinking is from God's perspective.
- Our cocoon? Christ wrapped us in His righteousness, and we emerged new creatures whose life is "in Christ!"

Transformers are co-laborers with Christ

In Acts 1:1, the Scripture reads *"all that Jesus began to **do** and **teach...**"*
As believer-priests, we are co-laborers with Christ His missions are now to be carried through us, all of us! He came to:

- Destroy the works of Satan.
- To enlarge Christ kingdom on earth.

Many of our local churches are not trying to destroy the works of Satan; they are more interested in a pact of co-existence and assimilation. It seems all their activities are birthed "under the sun" and are therefore earthy. It's God's will that we be *holy* examples of righteousness for Kingdom reality and power against the works of Satan through prayer and obedience to the *absolute* truth of God's Word. Jesus said, "These signs shall follow them that believe ......" In other words, the concern is not what we can do in our own strength – but what God can do through us if we submit to His will. We must know Him in order to know His will. It doesn't make sense to keep preaching about the "power of the Gospel" and Kingdom expansion," but never witnessing the reality of it! We have got to be bold, repent and renew our minds." Notice God's Word:

- Saves
- Heals
- Preserves

- Delivers
- And so much more

God's truth will set you free (see John 8:32). However, that's only for those Christians who abide [dwell / live] in the Word of God because that is the way the Spirit reveals the truth. It is the truth we know that sets us free!

Recent Barna research reflects that just over three quarters or (77%) of Americans "believe the values and morals of America are swiftly declining. When asked what is to blame for the decline 32% attribute the shift to a lack of Bible reading. Notice the blessings upon those who experience the reality of God's absolute truth, they:

- *Experience* the love of the Father, the Son and the Holy Spirit
- *Experience* the joy of obedience and service.
- *Experience* more holiness [separation to].
- *Experience* separation from the bondage of sin.
- *Experience* right relationship and true fellowship with God the Father and Christ the Son.
- *Experience* the fruit and gifts of the Holy Spirit
- *Experience* a right relationship and true fellowship with others.
- *Experience* His protection from sin.

God's truth will *sanctify* you (see John 17:17). Jesus prayed the Father sanctify [set apart/cleanse] them [disciples of all ages] through His truth. It is refreshing to know that despite the varying opinions and experiences of people untrustworthy as they are – God's Word is always true! We can know absolute Truth!

The alternative

If we agree with and walk after the course of this world, we die. But, if we

live and walk through the conviction and power of the Holy Spirit, we repent, and walk in the Spirit as citizens of the kingdom of Heaven. We have eternal life. Our *thoughts* lead the way.

God intends for us to use our minds as I said earlier as instruments in moving into a Christlike mind-set. There is an old saying concerning computers, "Garbage in garbage out." We should be careful about what goes into our minds because it determines the direction of our lives.

The Scripture admonishes, *"Set your minds on things above, not on earthly things"* (Colossians 3:2).

> *"Whatever is true, whatever is noble,*
> *whatever is right, whatever is pure,*
> *whatever is lovely, whatever is admirable*
> *if anything is excellent or praiseworthy*
> *think on these things"*
> (Philippians 4:8)

"But God has revealed them to us through His Spirit. For the Spirit searches all things, yes, the deep things of God. For what man knows the things of a man except the spirit of the man which is in him? Even so no one knows the things of God except the Spirit of God. Now we have received, not the spirit of the world, but the Spirit who is of God, that we might know the things that have been freely given to us by God. These things we also speak, not in words which man's wisdom teaches but which the Holy Spirit teaches comparing spiritual things with spiritual. But the natural man does not receive the things of the Spirit of God, for they are foolishness to him, nor can he know them, because they are spiritually discerned. But he who is spiritual judges all things, yet he himself is rightly judged by no one. For "who has known the mind of the Lord that he may instruct Him?" But we have the mind of Christ" (1 Corinthians 2:10-16). Through the Holy Spirit and the Word, we can have the mind of Christ.

Satan pushes for self-satisfaction

Hear, O earth: behold, **I will certainly bring calamity on this people, even the fruit of their thoughts,** *because they have not heeded My words, nor My law, but rejected it* (Jeremiah 6:19). Emphasis added.

One of Satan's primary distractors is to prevent us from *thinking* about the preciousness of God, Christ, heaven and eternal things there. He lures us through his temptations in three areas which make up our old sin nature: *the lust of the flesh, the lust of the eyes, and the pride of life.* This was his strategy with Eve (see Genesis 3:6, 13) and with Jesus (see Luke 4:1-13 and Matthew 4:1-11). If we yield to the cravings of the old sin nature, its lust and desires, we will seek for *self*-satisfaction and *self*–glorification which brought Lucifer down. With this thinking and appeal:

- We will never be like Christ if we cannot *think* like Christ. "As a man thinks in his heart, so is he" (see Proverbs 23:7).
- Our treasures dictate what we *think*. Jesus said, "Where your treasure is, there will your heart be also" (see Matthew 6:21). Paul said, "Set your affection on things above, not on the things on the earth" (Colossians 3:2).
- We cannot *think* like Christ until we learn to love what He loves and only what He loves. Jesus said to the Pharisees, "You are those who justify yourselves before men, but God knows your hearts. For what is *highly esteemed* among men is an abomination in the sight of God" (see Luke 16:15). Emphasis added throughout.

Don't let the devil deceive you; whatever we *think* about continually is what we love. It doesn't matter what it is. If it is of this world or "under the sun" as Solomon puts it, it is temporary, and is hindering us from *thinking* about Christ.

> "Love not the world, or the things that are in the world. If anyone loves the world, the love of the Father is not in him. For all that is in the world, the lust of the flesh, the lust of the eyes, and the pride of life, is not of the Father, but is of this world. And the world is passing away, and the lust of it: but he [or she] who does the will of God abides forever" (1 John 2:15-17). Emphasis added.

John was alluding to the three different ways believers could be lured away from loving God (see Genesis 3:6).

1. The lust of the flesh refers to desires for sinful sensual pleasure.
2. The lust of the eyes refers to covetousness or materialism.
3. The pride of life refers to being proud of one's position in this world.

Satan seems to be highly successful at using these ploys; therefore, much of America is characterized by these three lusts today. Remember:

> "Do not be deceived,
> God is not mocked,
> for whatever

a man sows
that he
will also reap.
For he that sows
to his flesh
shall of the flesh
reap corruption,
but he that sows
to the Spirit
shall of the Spirit
reap everlasting life"
– (Galatians 6:7, 8)

Today the Christian Community is plagued with many people who think
that though he or she sows to their *flesh,* they will [some how] escape the harvest of destruction and judgment that comes to those who practice sin, in fact many try to hide behind a misuse of grace as an easy out (Again see Galatians 5:19-21).

Of course, Satan is pleased with such thinking that keeps us from walking in the power of the Holy Spirit. He knows it is the power of God within that gives us the victory over sin and our sinful nature. When Satan is able to tempt us and we yield to our old sinful nature, Christians will do many things they should not do. In fact, they will act no different than the average person in the world and sometimes even worse. This also causes us to show indifference and lack of interest and do not the things that we should.

Great expectations

Christian character is not mere moral and legal correctness, but it is the possession and manifestation of nine graces [fruit of the Spirit]:

Character of the inward state

- Love – esteem, devotion, mutuality (v. 22; 1 Corinthians 13; Romans 8:28)
- Joy – rejoice even among the worse circumstances (v. 22; Philippians 4:11)

- Peace – keep your heart and mind without anxiety (v. 22; Philippians 4:7)

Character in expression toward others

- Longsuffering – power under control (v. 22; II Corinthians 6:3-10)
- Goodness – kindness, patience (v. 22; Romans 15:14; II Thessalonians 1:11)
- Kindness – goodness, patience (v. 22; 1 Corinthians 13:4)

Character in expression toward God

- Faith – faithful, faith (v. 22; 3:10)
- Meekness – gentleness, submission, teachable (v. 22; II Corinthians 10:1)
- Self-control – temperance, self-mastery (I Corinthians 7:9; 1:23, 31)

This portrait of Christ's character is a definition of "fruit" in (John 15:1-8). This character is produced in the believer through his or her vital union in Christ. The fruit of the Spirit is manifested in those believers who are yielded to Him (see John 15:5; 1 Corinthians 12:12, 13, Galatians 5:22, 23).

All New Testament believer-priests should live so far above the world as to not need to seek its pleasures, and therefore they will recommend true Christianity to the world as the source of the highest happiness on earth. The believers' love for God and Christ, their peaceful look, joyful countenance, and their experiencing cheerfulness regardless of circumstances impacts the unsaved and the saved.

When Moses was in God's presence on the mount, he picked up some of God's glory so that his face shone when he returned to the camp (see Exodus 34:29-35). Moses was not radiating glory from within – he was only reflecting that he had seen on the mount.

But the glory on Moses' face eventually faded. It was temporary. He had to put a veil over his face so that the people could not see the fading glory (see 2 Corinthians 3:13). Instead of veiling our faces, we want the world to see what the grace of God can do in the lives of Christians. We have absolutely nothing to hide!

"But we all, with unveiled face, beholding as in a mirror the glory of the Lord, are being transformed into the same image from glory to glory, just as by the Spirit of the Lord" (2 Corinthians 3:18).

"But the path of the just is like the shining sun, that shines even brighter unto the perfect day" (Proverbs 4:18).

However, the progressive, pleasure loving, and pleasure-seeking members regard this life as impractical and bondage. The trick of Satan is to get people thinking more highly of themselves, their material goods, and their affairs than they think of God and His will. We become like the God we worship (see Psalm 115:8).

Christ our Example

Wrong teaching has improperly defined the Kingdom of God and how it works. Some teach that the Kingdom of God is for some time in the future, but not in the here and now. But Jesus taught and demonstrated that the Kingdom of God is a present-day reality. It exists now in the invisible realm and is superior to everything in the visible realm. There are ungodly people working in the Christian communities for the sole purpose of "dumbing down" the churches.

Secular humanists and atheists are delivering a very strong message that denies absolute truth, the supernatural, God and the things of God. This teaching is of the devil, and it is amazing that so many people for personal reasons would rather believe a lie than humble themselves under a Holy God. Man is determined to be the measure of all things and has no need for the true God.

Many of us have preached in the name of Jesus without any demonstration of power. Yet we see very readily that the mark of Jesus' and the early church's preaching and teaching was "with great power." Jesus promised that we would do even greater things.

Again, that did not mean under our own power and strength, but He promised, that we would receive power after the Holy Spirit has come upon us (see Acts 1:8). The promise of the Holy Spirit was fulfilled at Pentecost and He is still here in us!

REFLECTION AND DISCUSSION QUESTIONS: CHAPTER 13

1. The Greek word for transform means to _____ _____.

2. Anything you put above God and His _____ is idolatry.

3. Paul's use of the word "flesh" referred to the entire _____ _____.

4. We must become _____ [learners] of the truth.

5. Discuss our becoming like the _____ we worship.

6. I can apply this lesson to my life by:

7. Closing Statement of Commitment:

SECTION VI

Get the Real Thing

CHAPTER FOURTEEN

Controlled by the Love of Christ

"For the love of Christ compels me, because we judge thus: that if One died for all, then all died; and He died for all, that those who live should live no longer for themselves, but for Him who died for them and rose again"
(2 Corinthians 5:14, 15).

Paul said the love of Christ controls him, and likewise us because we have reached the conclusion that Christ died for all and all have died; and He died for all, that those who live might no longer live for themselves but for Him who for their sake died and was raised.

The love of Christ holds Paul on one end and keeps him from considering any alternatives. Fear of punishment, or expectation of reward are not factoring toward his decision; he is just overwhelmed by Christ's love for him! It is important for us to realize the same results: a response of gratitude and love toward Christ should compel us to not live for ourselves but for Him who loved us and gave Himself for us.

The Pauline and the General Epistles are filled with imperatives that command us to pursue holiness, Christlike character, and present our bodies living sacrifices. These imperatives are always based on Christ's finished work of living a sinless life, suffering a sin-bearing death and a glorious resurrection. This gives desire to duty.

Reality of the Christian life

The reality is that even as we come and desire more to do our duty, we continue experiencing the war between the flesh and the spirit. Those who are honest can identify with Paul's words such as:

"For what I am doing, I do not understand. For what I will to do, that I do not practice; but what I hate that I do" (Romans 6:15).

"I find then a law, that evil is present with me, the one who wills to do good" (Romans 7:21).

The question arises how do we remain motivated as the tension grows between flesh and spirit? We must keep our eyes on the glorious truth of the present reality, our justification, and righteous standing in Christ. Only then will we remain motivated to keep pursuing holiness. Too many Christians are depending on their own performance [works/ legalism] rather than the grace [unmerited favor] of God plus nothing, by which we were justified through believing in the Lord Jesus Christ and His work on the cross in the first place.

We can take absolutely no credit whatsoever for salvation. Grace is God's idea! It can't be worked for – nor can it be earned. It is a gift from God:

"For it is by grace you have been saved, through faith, and that not of yourselves, it is the gift of God, not of works, lest anyone should boast" (Ephesians 2:8-9).

As stated earlier, because Jesus was totally sinless, He was legally eligible to pay the penalty for all my sins [*past, present, and future*]. God has legally declared me innocent! Not guilty! Righteous! Because of Christ's finished work on the cross, I am now in "right standing" before God. He loves and accepts me. All He asks for in return is my love and trust in His Son.

This same righteousness of Christ *"deposited to my account"* is available free to you and everyone else who believes in and receives Christ as their personal Savior. Christ voluntarily came down from heaven to take the punishment for sin that we deserve.

We did absolutely nothing to deserve His love, grace and mercy. Yet He died for the whole world! He reached down to us – not us reaching up to Him! I treasure the words of an old hymn of the church, "Nothing in my hands I bring simply to the cross I cling."

The glory of witnessing

In Acts 1:8 Jesus said, "You shall be My witnesses …." The word "shall" carry with it command authority. We are commanded to witness for the Lord, but not until we are equipped by the Holy Spirit. Once He has come upon the believer, he or she shall receive power [to witness]. He is also the Spirit of truth who will lead us into all truth. It is the truth of the gospel that saves people.

Therefore, those believers with the truth can witness the same to others, who hear and believe the truth about Christ accept it and by faith witness to yet others. The Lord is pleased and receives glory when we work in this manner and when we do so as gospel witnesses. Everything we are and everything we do is from the outflow of God's love and mercy delivered to us by the body and blood of Jesus.

Many Christians individually and corporately are buying into the secular belief that our beliefs are our own and should not be shared with others. Those who adhere to this error are probably missing their greatest opportunity to introduce the gospel to those without Christ.

We should see our workplace and other secular environments as opportunities to build meaningful friendships that can introduce those in our area of influence to the gospel that has saved us and has made us happy and productive citizens. By and large we have the privilege of demonstrating the gospel and power in a transformed life.

REFLECTION AND DISCUSSION QUESTIONS: CHAPTER 14

1. We are to pursue _____, Christlike character and present our bodies as _____ _____.

2. Performance rather than _____ by which we were _____.

3. Briefly explain Acts 1:8 in relation to my personal witnessing:

4. Everything we are and do is from an outflow of _____ love and _____ delivered to us by the body and blood of Jesus.

5. A transformed life demonstrates the _____ and its _____.

6. I can apply this lesson to my life by:

7. Closing Statement of Commitment.

CHAPTER FIFTEEN

Radically Bold in Life

"Let love be without hypocrisy. Abhor what is evil. Cling to what is good"
(Romans 12:9).

The spirits of this age are bold and aggressive and yet, subtle and deceptive. As followers of Christ we must affirm that which is truly good and present in every human culture. At the same time, we must be very discerning as the very opposite is also true. The problem is that unless we are very sensitive to God and able to wisely discern the so-called blurred boundaries between right and wrong or holy and unholy, culture can have just as much effect on us as we have on it. How can this happen, you may ask? Research shows that spiritual and biblical illiteracy has taken a sharp rise upward over the past several decades in our society and too many churches.

Persecution

The saying, ignore history and it will repeat itself, seems to be true and on the horizon globally. The Church has recorded many periods in its history wherein Christians were persecuted for their faith; and many were sent to horrible deaths because they would not deny Christ. The Roman Empire dominated the known world as the only world superpower at that time and officially a pagan nation in nature. Seeking *unity,* the emperor Domitian had made Christianity illegal during his reign from AD 81 to 96.[13]

Persecution broke out for the second time in AD 95. The Jews had refused to pay a poll tax for the support of Capitolinus Jupiter. It was during this persecution that the apostle John was exiled to the Isle of Patmos where he wrote the Book of Revelation. The persecution seemed to intensify the spread of the faith rather than stop it.

The anti-Christian spirit grew so great that killing Christians turned into a sporting event. The first organized persecution, which resulted from definite governmental policy, took place in Bithynia during the governorship of Pliny the Younger about 112. Supposedly, no Christians were to be sought out; but if someone reported that a certain person was a Christian, the Christian was to be punished *unless* he or she recanted and worshiped the gods of the Romans. Looking at the growing oppression toward religious freedom – through neglect history is being repeated. The Roman governor's main claim for the persecution was the *sellers* of sacrificial animals were impoverished as a result of the fast-growing Christianity.

Think of the cost when Christian silversmiths *refused* to make the pagan images the people worshiped. Christian homes were broken up; unemployment among Christians grew because they refused to say, "Caesar is lord" but continuously proclaimed "Jesus is LORD!" Many Christians during that period considered it a privilege to die for Christ. How far are we from that kind of hatred for Christians in this country?

Periodically, we hear of some one or a group in the Middle East or Africa making a death decision rather than deny their faith in Christ Jesus. Here in America Christians are intimidated or persecuted in many areas by an infusion of secular laws, many of which you will never know exist until they begin to affect you personally. As America continues to pursue and adapt the LBGTQ agenda at the cost of "we the people." Even at our best, we still fall so short when we reject the truth and wisdom of God's Word in our planning and decision-making. Think of the terror of a young mother having to send her young son into a male gender only restroom as she can no longer take him into the [female gender] bathroom with her. Rather than calling this issue a civil rights matter which it is not, we should realize that it is a clear attempt to advance the hedonistic and secular humanism agenda.

Religious liberty in America

In a recent poll a higher priority on preserving the religious freedom of Christians than for other faith groups ranking the Muslim faith as the least deserving according to a new survey. However, the percentages varied dramatically when the respondents were asked about specific faith traditions. The polls reflected:

- 82% of respondents said, religious liberty protections were important for Christians.
- 61% said the same for Muslims.
- 7 in 10 said religious liberty was important for the Jewish faith.

- 67% said so of Mormons.
- People who identified with no religion were ranked about even with Muslims.[14]

"Religious freedom is now in the eyes of the beholder."
– Charles Haynes, Director of the Religious Freedom Center[15]

My wife and I have traveled and ministered on four continents over the years and have experienced people suppressed because of a national religion to the exclusion of all others. Please believe me when I say religious freedom is a blessing to be cherished. If we continue our present course of ignoring the attacks against Christianity; how long will it take to bring down Christianity in this country? Consider the fact that most church leaders seem oblivious of what's happening or undoubtedly suffering from "ostrich syndrome!" Satan is concentrating his forces on the foundational doctrine of Christianity and taking down America in the collateral damage. This is a culture war to be sure, but *it is also a spiritual war.* Who are the players behind the scene? Christianity is now persecuted in all major institutions in America, especially in media, academia, social engineering, special interests, and government. We can take the history of the early church as a guide. The problem of obedience to Christ or Caesar has been present in every age of the Church since its inception.

America's strategy seems to be to adopt the old saying, ["If you can't beat them, join them!"] but that is not an option here. Believe it or not it's either Christ or Caesar – not both! It seems that the goal of the new tolerance is to make us all "one." However, the tolerance is geared [agree with us or you will be cast out] – many of our churches are amending their constitutions and by-laws to accommodate come what may – all in the name of inclusivity. We have a tendency of legalizing those problems that we can't handle in this country. In a major evening newscast, a couple of years back, it was reported that accidents resulting from marijuana intoxication has moved upward from 42 to 84% in areas where the drug has been legalized for recreational purposes – morning newspaper will show how irresponsible that conclusion was. There was a time when the pagan would say enough is enough and support deterrents put into place for public safety, today sinful pleasure and more things are the priorities.

Our Federal Government has over the years imposed secular laws upon us that defy God's biblically recorded moral laws. The enactment of these laws makes clear the stated fact that, "there are active secular [demonically energized] people in this country bent on destroying it."

The power of just one atheistic judge and the non-elected special interest groups have eliminated "we the people" and it seems the system of "checks and balances" between the three branches of the government has been deactivated. Without "we the people" the United States of America is a democracy in name only.

God wants a separated people

If the Church caves-in to the culture, it would really be yielding to the world, the flesh, and the devil. God's pattern works on the *principle* of separation unto Himself only those persons who have experienced a second birth, "born from above" in Christ Jesus (see John 3:16; Romans 10:9, 10). He has made salvation the basic pattern for entering the Christian life and blessing. That may sound foreign in a day when "inclusivity" which seems to be the cultural watchword; but this separation or exclusivity is Scripturally based. The power of God is released in our lives when we live a separated life in the sense, He means it. There is a real danger to our souls when we do not exercise our faith as He desires in this life.

The point of this separation goes back to the very beginning; God had laid down the *principle* that His people would be a separated people – unto Him! That *meant and means* total dependence on Him for everything! "We can do all things through Christ who strengthens us," however, we should be reminded of another Scriptural passage. Jesus said, "Without Me you can do nothing." After Adam and Eve sinned, and Cain killed his brother Abel – Seth was born, and men began to call upon the name of the Lord (see Genesis 4:26). However, these were not the only people in the world. Cain also became the father of a considerable people group. Eventually these two groups intermarried. We read the results of such a union in Genesis 6:

And it came to pass, when men began to multiply on the face of the earth, and daughters were born unto them, that the sons of God saw the daughters of men that they were fair; and they took them wives of all which they chose. And the Lord said, "My Spirit shall not always strive with man, for that he also is flesh" (Genesis 6:1-3).

The intermarriages between the godly line of Seth and the ungodly line of Cain were overwhelmingly evil which brought the judgment of the flood; and God starting over with faithful Noah and his off springs. The same principle is seen in the lives of:

Abraham

When Abram [later Abraham] was separated by the Lord (see Genesis 12:1, 2), he took his father, Tarah with him. Partial obedience is disobedience. God wouldn't let Abraham go into the land but stopped the families in Haran where they lived for 15 years until the death of Tarah. When Abraham left Haran, he had his nephew Lot with him, but God's fullest blessing did not come until he was separated from Lot. Strife between the two groups of herdsmen caused this separation according to pattern.

Undoubtedly the strife between their herdsmen alerted Abraham to the fact that he was not fully obedient to God. Abraham and Lot separated themselves completely (see Genesis 13:9-11). God does not necessarily call on us to separate from our loved ones, but in the case of Abraham, He did.

After the separation God promised Abraham:

"Lift up thine eyes now, and look from the place where you are northward, southward, eastward, westward: For all the land which you see I give to you and your descendants forever. And I will make thy seed as the dust of the earth ……." (Genesis 13:14-16).

Israel

The same truth is seen in God's dealing with Israel. He called them out from among the nations to be a special people for Himself. Likewise, He called them forth out of Egypt [which is a type of the world]. While in Egypt the Israelites were not able to do the will of God. They had to be separated from Egypt. Solomon in his dedicatory prayer referred to this special separation by God when he said,

"For You separated them [Israel] from among all the peoples of the earth to be Your inheritance, as You spoke by Your servant Moses, when You brought our fathers out of Egypt, O Lord God" (1 Kings 8:53).

The sad truth of the matter is the people of Israel did not maintain this command and position of separation very long. Moses commented concerning God's dealing with Israel and their waywardness in his farewell to the nation:

"When the Most High divided their
inheritance to the nations,
When He separated the sons of Adam,
He set the boundaries of the peoples
According to the number of the
Children of Israel.
For the Lord's portion is His people;
Jacob is the place of His inheritance.
He found him in a desert land
And in the wasteland, a howling wilderness;
He encircled him, He instructed him,
He kept him as the apple of His eye,
As an eagle stirs up its nest,
Hovers over its young,
Spreading out its wings, taking
them up,
Carrying them on its wings,
So the Lord alone led him,
And there was no foreign god with him.
He made him ride in the heights of
the earth,
That he might eat the produce of the fields;
He made him draw honey from the rock,
And oil from the flinty rock."
– (Deuteronomy 7-13)

But Israel was not satisfied. The people did not stay separated. They began to worship strange gods; they sacrificed to demons, and God. They broke the line of separation between them and their heathen neighbors. God was forced to chastise them. A careful study of the Books of Joshua, Judges, and Kings shows that as long as Israel was *separated* to God they prospered. When they separated from Him, He forsook them. It finally led to the dispersion of the Northern nation and the Babylonian capture and exile of the Southern nation. Wake up America! We need revival!

REFLECTION AND DISCUSSION QUESTIONS: CHAPTER 15

1. In the Roman Empire many Christians were given the choice to worship _____ or _____.

2. In the name of "unity" Emperor Domitian made _____ illegal during his reign from AD 81 to 96.

3. Discuss how "we the people" has suffered as for as the laws of the land are concerned today along with the impact of humanistic politicians and judges are concerned:

4. From your reading of this chapter, what was determined to be the reason for the flood in Noah's day?

5. A study of the Books of Joshua, Judges, and Kings show that as long as Israel was _____ to God they prospered. How would that principle fit America today?

6. I can apply this lesson to my life by:

7. Closing Statement of Commitment:

SECTION VII

I Belong to Him

CHAPTER SIXTEEN

A New Humanity

"Salvation belongs to our God who sits on the throne and to the Lamb"
(Revelation 7:10).

God's love for His creatures is great and inexplicable; He wants a people for Himself. Thus, apart from Abraham, God chose his family through his son Isaac, and the next generation, his twelve sons to be the heads of the twelve tribes of Israel – His very own people; Israel was born as a nation. The theme of the Bible really is concerned with God's sovereign love for His creatures.

God had in mind from the beginning that Israel would serve as His witness to the world – showing humanity that idolatry and polytheism are abominations to Him. *Yahweh* was Israel's Hebrew name for their covenant God – and He alone is God. Israel was to:

- Render absolute love and devotion to Him.
- Live a life of holy obedience to His instructions (moral law).
- Show the rest of humanity how human life can be a bit of heaven, if lived in His will.

In the last chapter we saw how God delivered Israel from Egyptian bondage through the Red Sea by a show of His grace and mercy, and settled His free people as promised, in a land "flowing with milk and honey." On the way from Egypt at Mt. Sinai during the exodus God made a gracious covenant with Israel, constituting them as:

- His sons and daughters and giving them the right to call Him their God.
- He gave them His holy law.
- He made provision for them as sinful sons of Adam by giving them a sanctuary, sacrifices for sin, and a *separated* priesthood to minister "in things pertaining to God."

- He charged them strictly to keep in mind that He did not choose them because of any inherit superiority on their part, but He alone by His gracious election in love.
- He sent prophets to them with His holy Word, men who proclaimed His will to them, protesting their sin, and calling them back to their law and to their God who had given them both their law and their covenant status.

Even a shallow reading of the Old Testament makes clear that Israel failed terribly. We saw the end of both nations, Israel in the north and Judah in the south went down the same road of idolatry, immorality and social injustice. The results were the same, God's judgment.

The regrouping

What a joyous day it was when the Lord re-gathered His people, actually more from Judah than from Israel – yet a representative *remnant* from all twelve tribes and back in their land and around their rebuilt temple on Mount Moriah.

- Once more the daily sacrifices for sin were offered up.
- Israel was *forever* cured of all tendencies toward idolatry.
- However, Israel was not cured of the tendency to confuse holiness with legalism.
- Sadly, Jewish moralistic hairsplitting so shrouded over God's law until it was hardly recognizable.

Yet, despite all their unworthiness, God was still able to use His failing people for His glory. A great number of Gentiles from across the Greek-Roman world were so attracted to the God of Israel that they began to worship Him each Sabbath in the local synagogues of the Jews. In the Book of Acts, they are spoken of as the devout proselytes. These Gentiles along with such Jews as also repented at the preaching of Paul and other Christian leaders formed the nucleus in each faith community for the chain of congregations [a new humanity *"in Christ"*] which Paul and other apostles established across the empire of the first century era.

Thus, we see that the Christian church was nurtured initially in Judaism. *God had a faithful remnant in Israel, His ancient covenant people who* followed His leading and entered the new phase of His redemptive work according to pattern, the Church of the Living God in the world, but not of the world.

The new humanity ["in Christ"]

God always had His believing remnant, spanning from Abraham to Christ. And from Christ through His incarnation, public ministry, atoning death, and resurrection – God brought a new humanity into a new era; that is those who by faith in the finished work of Christ on Calvary have been "born from above" are and no longer of this world (see John 17:14).

Without regard to ethnicity He constituted the new humanity. Despite dangers and open threats as time passed more and more people "from every tribe and tongue and people and nation" in great numbers came into God's new people [the Church]. This was God's pattern and plan in action.

Most Jews failed to see the hand of God in the establishment of His new people; and even up to this present hour many have failed to claim the blessings which God willed for them to enjoy. Some of the first aspects of God's people serving as witnesses to the world are:

- A holy and happy people separated unto God.
- A free brother and sisterhood of forgiven and forgiving people.
- A blood-washed people who are rejoicing in the justification which God gave them in Christ and His finished work on Calvary.
- A special place for each other in their hearts.
- A "great leveling" is taking place so that the factors which in the unredeemed society break people into classes are wiped out. Rich and poor, young and old, cultured and uneducated, people of every race and nation: all are to be one joyous people made so by the love He pours into our hearts by the Holy Spirit (Romans 5:5).
- A regenerated people who are renewed in the Spirit of their minds so that:

  The dishonest become honorable
  The carnal become pure
  The hateful become loving
  The stingy become generous
  The self-centered become God and Christ-centered

This is a sober description of God's will for His church which is realized in Christ, insofar as the people are soundly converted to the mind of Christ through their response and humble submission to the Word of God and the Spirit of God. This is the kind of church which enjoys the evangelistic and teaching mission success in carrying out the great commission (see Matthew 28:19, 20). It is God's will that we:

- Die with Christ (to sin)
- Rise with Christ (to newness of life)
- Ascend with Christ (into the presence of God)
- Reign with Christ (by a life of victory in the kingdom of God)

This theme of the union of Christian believers with Christ is common throughout the New Testament. The Book of Ephesians sets it forth with special clarity:

"But God, who is rich in mercy, because of His great love with which He loved us, even when we were dead in trespasses made us alive together with Christ (by grace you have been saved), and raised us up together, and made us sit together in heavenly places in Christ Jesus, that in the ages to come He might show the exceeding riches of His grace in His kindness toward us in Christ Jesus" (Ephesians 2:4-7).

Salvation is for the glory of God as He puts His limitless mercy and love on display for those who are spiritually dead because of their sinfulness. A spiritually dead person needs to be made alive by God. It's the only way the dead can be made alive. Salvation then, is very much for the believer's blessing, but it is even more for the purpose of eternally *glorifying* God for bestowing on believers His endless and limitless grace and kindness. All of heaven glorifies Him for what He has done in saving sinners (Carefully study Ephesians 3:10; Revelation 7:10-12).

We were hopeless without Christ

In a day when humanity is trying to explain away the supernatural by claiming everything happens through the natural realm and the individual's own efforts; it is necessary that all Christians realize that although people are required to believe for salvation, even that faith is part of the gift of God which saves and cannot be exercised by one's own power. The Scripture explicitly explains,

*"For by grace
you have been saved
through faith,
and that not of yourselves,
it is the gift of God,
not of works,
lest anyone should boast"*
(Ephesians 2:8).

God's grace is preeminent in *every aspect* of salvation and the entire Christian life as well (Study Romans 3:10; Galatians 2:16).

REFLECTION AND DISCUSSION QUESTIONS: CHAPTER 16

1. From the beginning Israel was the servant of God's _____ to the world.

2. The Old Testament makes clear idolatry, immorality, and social injustice brought down the nations of _____ and _____.

3. A majority of Jesus failed to this day to see the hand of God in the establishment of a _____ _____.

4. God's grace is preeminent in every _____ of salvation.

5. Discuss the status of "repentance" in the local churches today: has it gone by the wayside in the American church today?

6. I can apply this lesson to my life by:

7. Closing Statement of Commitment:

CHAPTER SEVENTEEN

Quality Commitments

"Now when He was in Jerusalem at the Passover, on the feast day, many believed in His name, when they saw the miracles which He did. But Jesus did not commit Himself unto them, because He knew all men, and needed not that should testify of man: for He knew what was in man" (John 2:23-25).

There is an old saying, "all that glitters – is not gold!" So true especially in light of all the artificiality today, it certainly will be profitable for us to make a serious re-evaluation of the standards of commitment in our churches to make sure they are the authentic biblical and spiritual standards as set down in the truth of God's Word.

Quality control

During my long military career, I was used to quality control or final inspection of everything we repaired. After a piece of equipment was repaired prior to releasing it back to the outfit, it had to pass a through quality control inspection of the work completed and insure it was combat ready. In those days, the individual responsible for maintaining the helicopter or airplane rode on the aircraft as part of the crew, therefore quality control was always on board.

The quality control positions have been deleted in many areas of industry and many franchises due to downsizing, budget or other cuts in many organizations. These duties have been replaced with spot checks, trust and it seems in many cases – damage control! Therefore, many automobiles and other pieces of equipment are released with what may be shoddily rigged or incomplete repairs. So, we hear of wheels coming off cars and engines and other parts falling off aircrafts while in flight! In fact, a couple of years ago, an engine did fall from an aircraft within five miles of our home. The evening news reported a complete rear axle assembly came apart from an eighteen-wheeler on an interstate highway causing the trailer to flip over and collapse. Without the Holy Spirit, quality commitments for churches and her members are falling apart as secular and intellectual means are continuously tried and proven to be ineffective in the local assemblies.

This holds true also within churches and ministries where too often quantity takes precedence over quality. In this highly competitive age those *outward appearances* of "success" that are calculated to enhance the *reputation* of the preacher or the prestige of the institution, which are deemed to be of greater importance than the abiding biblical mission and ministries. In such unholy situations to get results, the end too often justifies the means. Many times, the means are questionable and to say the least – the results are extremely dubious. Without quality control in many such incidents – confrontation is simply a surface matter, because quantity still holds the precedence! Too bad we can't stand-down a church until all the bugs are worked out of, as has happened to the four hundred [grounded] Boeing 737 aircrafts.

Quality confrontation

Our churches are filled with much treating of the symptoms rather than digging deeper for the cause of the malady. It is much easier to confront a person with his or her *"sins"* than it is to confront the person with their *"sin."*

- *Sin* is an attitude which affects a person's fundamental relationship to God: it has to do with what a person *is*.
- Whereas *"sins"* have to do with what a person *does*, and we all have a tendency of being able to detach what we "do" from what we "are!"

We all excel with expertise in the art of justifying "self" and we can produce innumerable reasons as to why what we did was excusable – even if it was wrong! We can even feel almost virtuous, in accepting the blame for that which so obviously was *only* natural, and almost an inevitable expectation due to enticing, and provocative circumstances or people! For this very reason a person can admit to sinning and be sorry for what he or she has done – without *admitting* that what was done is result of what he or she *is*.

Therefore, a person may be called upon numerous times to face the lesser issues of what he or she has done – without *once* being confronted with the greater issue of what he or she is. So, for this person there is "comfort" in confession, freedom from fear, and *relief* to a bad conscience; all these together will eliminate for this individual any need for any basic change in their fundamental relationship with God. This is not according to God's pattern.

This kind of confession falls far short of true *repentance* – and rather than change, this kind of conduct and behavior toward the Lord has become the new norm for many [without heart] on the local churches' membership rolls. Moses had a similar situation with the children of Israel in the wilderness, his preaching reduced his people to tears again and again – but they remained in the wilderness!

- They had no heart for Canaan!
- There was no lack in response to Moses, but they would not do business with God!

The people were afraid of God's presence. The Scripture says, *"Now all the people witnessed the thunder, the lightning flashes, the sound of the trumpets, and the mountain smoking; and when the people saw it, they trembled and stood afar off." Then they said to Moses, "You speak with us, and we will hear; but let not God speak with us, lest we die"* (Exodus 20:18-19).

These people wanted Moses to be their mediator between them and God. They wanted second-hand religion. They wanted neither godlessness nor godliness. They did not know how to live, and they were afraid to die! Second-hand religion keeps many pastors in business and makes them indispensable to their congregations – but second-hand religion cannot "make disciples" (see Matthew 28:19-20):

- There will be no deliverance from the old nature.
- There will be no spontaneity of action in the people.
- There will be no evidence of the divine initiative in the people.
- There will be no total availability of the people to God.

True quality commitment

This type of (zero) relationship with God can be found in people from the pulpit to the door of the local churches, as more and more churches adopt forms of godliness and deny the power and presence of the Spirit of God. True quality commitment to the Lord Jesus Christ gives Him full "right of way," and He releases His life through us in all the fullness, freshness, and power of divine action, so that according to His gracious promise in John 7:38:

> *"He who believes in Me,*
> *as the Scripture has said,*
> ***"out of his heart***
> ***will flow***
> ***rivers of living water."***

The significance of Jesus' invitation centers in the fact that He was the fulfillment of all the Feast of Tabernacles anticipated. He was the One who provided the living water that gives eternal life to man (study John 4:10-11).

There is still much to be desired in the quality of commitment so needed today in the worldwide evangelistic outreach of the body of Christ denominationally and non-denominationally. Even more to our shame are those opportunities we get to practice deplorable hypocrisy in formal *public* acts of commitment to Christ so common with many Christians today. These acts are for the most part totally void of any spiritual content whatsoever and serve only to satisfy traditional commitments of religious observances in an otherwise godless society where:

- The Lord Jesus Christ is neither accepted as Savior nor honorably mentioned in the public square as Lord of all.
- Church approval has been granted by the majority; to the unwelcomed attention of those who would insist on a reality of spiritual experience.
- The unspiritual do not know what they believe, nor believe what they know.
- Many churches operate without a sense of mission – governed by boards riddled with infidelity.
- The worst enemies of the church are within their own ranks?

The Word of God to the Jews of Paul's day is well fitted for Christians today:

For *the name of God is blasphemed among the Gentiles because of you!* *For He is not a Jew who is one outwardly, nor is circumcision that which is outward in the flesh; but he is a Jew who is one inwardly; and circumcision is that of the heart, in the spirit, not in the letter; whose praise is not from men but from God"* (Romans 2:24, 28-29).

In a day when churches are divorcing themselves from the Cross and blood of Jesus, and the Holy Spirit and His gifts and ministries becoming hopelessly helpless; a clear understanding of this passage is timely and imperative. The change of heart that Paul describes with the image of inner circumcision conjured up or faked for it is the work of the Holy Spirit, not the result of external obedience to the Law. In fact, God *condemns* external observances, if they are not the product of a righteous heart.

REFLECTION AND DISCUSSION QUESTIONS: CHAPTER 17

1. "Sin" is an attitude which affects a person's fundamental relationship with God; it has to do with what a person _____.

2. "Sins" have to do with what a person _____.

3. We all excel in the art of justifying "self" and we are experts at giving reasons why what we did is excusable even if it was _____.

4. We live in a day when churches are divorcing the _____ _____.

5. The change of heart that Paul describes with the image of inner circumcision is the _____ of the _____ _____.

6. I can apply this lesson to my life by:

7. Closing Statement of Commitment:

SECTION VIII

Standing on the Promises

CHAPTER EIGHTEEN

Prove What the Will of God Is

*"Present your bodies as a living sacrifice; holy and acceptable
to God ....that you may prove what the will of God is"*
(Romans 12:1-2).

"Your bodies" in this passage refers to our whole selves, not merely our physical body. For fifteen hundred years the people of Israel had previously worshipped God by giving dead sacrifices. But since Jesus finished His work on Calvary, God's will is that we dedicate ourselves as living sacrifices.

During these perilous times we find that living for God requires as much faith and courage as dying a martyr's death. In this total dedication to God, we learn what His will is. The will of God is far more than a mere intellectual concept that we can learn in the classroom. It is living heart conviction!

We haven't arrived, but we've left

Believers first make the commitment to the Lord; and then enter their journey. We prove the will of God on the way. Living in the will of God is not like taking a guided tour, which begins with a detailed plan of travel outlined by a travel agent whose sources route you around the hazards, road construction and repairs, select the best hotels, restaurants and key sights along the way.

The Christians' journey through life begins with a hope and then a setting out. There is a goal – but the road is not marked in many places. Travelers *learn as they go along led of the Spirit and the Word.*

When the apostle Paul wrote to the Roman Christians, he could not have known that his trip to Jerusalem was going to be a disaster. He was going on the Lord's promise that he would go to Rome. Paul suffered many things, and many would say, "He was in the wrong place at the wrong time." We know though for the sake of the gospel, Paul would not agree. When reality fell on him in Jerusalem, however, he did not abandon his mission. He journeyed on to Rome, but he went in chains (study carefully Acts 27-28). Notice his motive:

"But I want you to know, brethren, that the things which happened to me have actually turned out for the furtherance of the gospel, so that it has become evident to the whole palace guard, and to all the rest, that my chains are in Christ; and most of the brethren in the Lord, leaving become confident by my chains, are much more bold to speak the word without fear" (see Philippians 1:12-14).

Paul wanted the Philippians to know that his imprisonment was advancing not hindering the gospel. These words comforted the Philippians who were concerned about his welfare. Secondly his words assured them that their prayers for him and the gifts they sent him were not in vain. Further he wrote,

"And I am sure that he who began a good work in you will complete it until the day of Jesus Christ" (1:6).

He stated his plans, but others modified them causing many unseen dangers toils and snares. For example, the trip to Rome which normally took two weeks, took them seven months. Salvation is by grace through faith; we do not achieve salvation by our works. But like Paul those who know Christ's redemption join in the work. So,

"Work out your own salvation
with fear and trembling.
for
it is God who works
in you
both to will and to do
His
good pleasure"
– (2:12-13).

God promises to work with and within us. "Now to Him who is able to do exceedingly abundantly above all that we ask or think, according to the power that works in us, to Him be glory in the church by Christ Jesus to all generations, forever and ever, Amen" (Ephesians 3:20-21).

No place for the novice

He promises in Romans 12:2 that we can "prove" what the will of God is. The Greek word for prove is *dokimazo* meaning "to test" or "shall try" KJV with the expectation of approving (also see I Corinthians 3:13). With the culture glued to feelings, fairness and self, most people would tend to think that the person must be reaping the harvest of some sin he or she has committed. This is not a situation for a novice, because cultural thought would cause them to cave-in. As we look at Paul in the Scriptures above, he did not necessarily know what was going to happen moving from one situation to the next – but he *knew* God, and that is most important in learning His will.

- The Lord wants us to love Him and let Him reveal Himself to each of us (see Matthew 6:33).
- He expects us to adjust our lives to Him (see John 15:4).
- He wants to work through us – but a right relationship with Him comes first and foremost (see Romans 5:10).
- He can do this only if we totally surrender to Him in humble dependency upon Him.

The question for most is what is God's will for my life? The real question to ask is, "What is God's will?" It was God's will for Paul to go to Rome, (carefully study chapters 27-28 of the Book of Acts). An old hymn of the church *The Lord will make a way somehow"* says,

"Like a ship that's tossed and driven
Battered by an angry sea,
When the storms of life are raging
And their fury falls on me,
I wonder what I have done
That makes this race so hard to run,
Then I say to my soul
Take courage
The Lord will make a way
Somehow!"

As we navigate these perilous times, like the songwriter and Paul, we can take courage for we know "the Lord will make a way somehow." I have every reason to believe that Paul like Job and many other men and women used of God was not necessarily told why (concerning the things they went through in their storms).

In spite of today's "feeling and seeing culture," which has infiltrated many of the local churches – one of the greatest developments of our own personal faith in God is that, while we are in the midst of a raging storm, we still muster up the courage to look people straight in their eyes and say, "I know the Lord will make a way!" Think about it He created this storm ...... these waves, these winds. I belong to Him and He belongs to me!" The chorus to the old hymn continues,

The Lord will make a way some-how, when beneath the cross I bow;
He will take away each sorrow; let Him have your burdens now;
When the load bears down so heavy; the weight is shown upon my brow,
There's a sweet relief in knowing,
O The Lord will make a way somehow!

REFLECTION ND DISCUSSION QUESTIONS: CHAPTER 18

1. We are to _____ our _____ as _____
   _____.

2. Living a holy life today may require much _____ and
   _____ as dying a martyr's death.

3. The will of God is more than an intellectual concept. It is a
   living _____.

4. Paul suffered _____ _____ for the sake
   of the gospel.

5. Prove means "to _____" with the expectation of
   approving.

6. I can apply this lesson to my life by:

7. Closing Statement of Commitment:

CHAPTER NINETEEN

Stand

"Do you not know that friendship with the world is enmity with God? Whoever therefore wants to be a friend of the world makes himself [or herself] an enemy of God"
(see James 4:4).

We live in a day when many local churches are more concerned with partisan politics, feelings, and the opinions of the majority, than the Holy Spirit and the truth of God's Word. They think it normal to let the world hold sway over them, knowing that to do so actually make you friends of the world. This verse is not speaking of God's attitude toward the believer – but the believer's attitude toward God.

The difference between the world and God is so vast that as we move toward the world, we alienate ourselves from God. In the world, sin is considered acceptable and pleasurable. Ultimately the world has lost its very awareness of sin – therefore to many in the world sin is all there is, a normal part of life?

Stand!

Satan knows that if he can get a foothold in any area of your mind – like a cancer, he can quickly attack and contaminate the other areas that are weak and needing to be strengthened by the Holy Spirit and the Word of God. Once he's in, his specialty is to corrupt your mind. He will instantly move to seize any area of your mind or emotions by bringing in active strongholds to counter spiritual growth and fruit-bearing. That's why we must immediately deal with any sin detected in our lives. Watch out for:

- Denial and unbelief
- Various strongholds
- Wrong thinking

- Wrong believing
- Generational fears, sins, and superstitions transferred from parents, family and others.
- Memories of terrible events that happened prior to salvation
- Incorrect teaching and training of doctrinal truths
- Things [other gods]
- Return to the law

We must remember the natural mind is enmity toward God; because we were all born with a rebellious nature against God inherited from Adam. Satan wants to keep Christians off balance! It is essential that we renew our minds through the truths of God's Word in order to stand against the wiles of the devil. Not only will the truth set you free, but your family also when applied correctly!

Our times

Paul cautions, "Don't live the way you use to live – the way the unsaved lives." The story goes some teenaged boys came across a man holding the reins with what had to be an old horse. Making fun of the animal, the boys quipped. "What does that old horse do, can he run?" "Can he do tricks?" Laughter! "What can he do?" The old man looked them straight in the eyes and said, "He can stand!"

When the church was born on the Day of Pentecost, history records a world very similar to ours. National borders were being removed as homelands were invaded and occupied by the Roman Army, violence against Christians became entertainment and Godly morals in the empire were almost non-existent.

Satanic interference was behind these activities then, just as it is today as we witness the determined efforts of radical Islam to destroy the Church of Jesus Christ in its very earliest settings in the Middle East. I see these present perilous days in America as a prelude of much worse things to come! Unless America repents and turns back to God, "Why should God allow us to go on boasting of past tense greatness?"

Partisan politics on a world-wide scale, the rise and fall of the Taliban, home-grown sleeper-groups and other radical elements seem to be our future, as biblical revelation goes on totally ignored by government leaders and a growing list of churches. Too few public or church officials anywhere in the USA are bold enough to *stand on the truths of God's Word* that they know – concerning the sexual immorality that's holding this country in its clutches today. Churches are not hearing what the Spirit is saying to them today.

The secular consensus seems to be winning many battles as they rule the media, education, science and reason, based on the false assumption that man, not God is the measure of all things. The battle lines are drawn and the battle for the minds of America is raging daily. Casualties are being claimed on every hand. The outcome of every person's life is being weighed upon the scale of acceptable "worship and service" especially during satanic attacks and times of temptation.

In the midst of the battle to whom will you bow, God or Satan?

It is imperative that true worship and service come forth now in the context of our daily living. We must be conditioned through the Holy Spirit and the truth of God's Word, if we are to *stand* – if we can't stand during the mere skirmishes that we face today, any survival as conditions grow worse, it is necessary for believers to build themselves up in the most holy faith for it will be impossible to stand without prior Spiritual and biblical preparation.

At times in the Old and New Testament, God through the man or woman of God had to call on the people to make a choice. Time and again the line of demarcation has been drawn between those who "serve the beast and bow to his image" and those who "worship and serve" the True and Living God. In Revelation 18:4 God is saying, *"Come out of her, My people, lest you share in her sins, and lest you receive of her plagues."* According to "pattern" God calls for His children to disentangle themselves from this evil world system – and return to full faith in the Savior. The judgment on our evil society living in sinful, arrogant, self-indulgence can be avoided – if we repent and turn back to God, now!

Who is on the Lord's Side?

We can take a lesson from the Israelites. The Lord had a "Call to Worship" in the wilderness. So Moses said, "The Lord God of the Hebrews has sent me to you saying, "Let My people go, that they may serve Me in the wilderness; but indeed, until now you would not hear" (see Exodus 7:16).

When Moses first spoke of God's love for the Israelites, we read that they "bowed low and worshipped" (see Exodus 4:13). But when trials or persecution came, they quickly began murmuring, complaining, and unscrupulous rebellion. That led to very shallow worship without heart. This same shallowness prevails in much of our Christian worship today:

- When the message speaks of God's love and care for His people, we bow low and worship.
- When the pressures of daily living arise, when temptations come, how quick we are to rebel against God.
- Without true worship in the human spirit, the soul has no protection of God!

God's purpose in the wilderness was to perfect true worship, which is based on the reality of God and not our circumstances. The Lord knows that the heart that will worship Him in the wilderness of affliction will continue to worship in the promised land of plenty. What comes out of our hearts during times of stress and temptation was hidden there during the pleasant times.

A child shall lead them

Our present-day society is just wrong! We now have a generation fully grown, who were raised up with "no absolutes" or "spiritual moral truth" and characterized by:

- Ungodliness
- Immorality
- Idolatry
- And nothing is safe

The sad news is things are getting worse not better. In many ways the state of the church culture is about the same. What is the solution? Well we can go to the Book of Daniel and follow the lead of four teenagers.

Daniel

The Book of Daniel emphasizes the sovereignty of God in the affairs of nations. It is important that we notice the similarity between the sad condition of Judah and America. Similar sins characterized Judah as stated concerning this country above:

- Disobedience
- Immorality
- Ungodliness
- Idolatry

Jerusalem did not fall merely because Nebuchadnezzar was strong – but because God had judged the people of Judah for their disobedience and idolatry. Daniel, Shadrach, Meshach and Abednego were God's champions, selected by the Chaldeans because of their royalty, knowledge and good looks to become Chaldeans by changing their names, eating food dedicated to idols.

But Daniel defied the king's order from the start by refusing to eat food and drink the wine from the king's table. He wouldn't chance eating food forbidden by the Law (see Leviticus 11). Carefully read these chapters, these four young men came to Babylon with convictions taught them by their parents:

1. Thoroughly taught and persuaded by their parents to stand on their convictions – these teens made a stand.
2. They loved and studied the Word of God.
3. They loved the Lord and were obediently devoted to Him.

We will stand true with our godly convictions if we are thoroughly convinced that they are true – we will not compromise:

- Holding to conviction will either destroy your character or build it.
- These four were godly examples to the other captives.
- Convinced that God would hear and answer their prayers.
- True to the Word of God (4:24-25).
- Three Hebrews refused to bow to the king's idol.

What convictions do you hold that guides your conduct? What convictions do you have that you are not willing to compromise? What about it, do you stand when threatened? People will usually compromise and fail due to one or more of the following:

- Fear
- Criticism
- Rejection
- Loss

We are entering days when we must be prepared to stand with unmovable godly convictions, or we will fail in times of temptation and persecution. For example, the Clerk of Court in North Carolina who refused to sign marriage licenses for same sex applicants due to her biblical convictions and beliefs.

Another case in point is the young couple who refused to prepare a wedding cake for a same sex marital reception; and as a result of their stand lost their business. When trouble comes, it's quite late to be trying to get prepared for it (study carefully 2 Timothy 3). Paul's letter to Timothy warning of perilous times written two thousand years ago reads like a morning newspaper any city USA today.

Parental love, caring, obedience and application of biblical teaching prepared Daniel, Meshach, Shadrach, and Abednego for the storm (Babylonian captivity) that was on the horizon. As I sit at my computer writing, the media is busy trying to prophesy the news by reporting what they perceive as news based on their evolutionary slant. At the same time end-time biblical prophecy is coming into clearer view with each passing day.

Biblically speaking, Paul prophesied two thousand years ago that many things we see shaping up day by day in these perilous times. Russia, a key player in the end times has made a move into Syria and partnering with Iran, and with very little effort they could be knocking on the door of Israel soon. It seems that America might be willing to make a deal. Are we willing to kick Israel to the curb? The candidates on neither side of the upcoming primaries are saying much about Israel's plight [Carefully study Ezekiel 38 and 39].

Each occurrence of a global crisis or potential crisis is reported by the media [with their slant on it] to strike fear in the hearts of the people of the world. Certainly, this will enhance the platform of the "man of sin" and his deception, simply because the people of the world are looking for *any reasonable* solution to their problems and from anywhere except God and the truth of His Word.

Yes, God is real!

The upcoming presidential primaries are already reflecting in the polls that this country has had its fill of politicians; and when translated, that probably means many of the people are about ready to accept almost anyone who is not connected with the Washington establishment. Hatred and contempt for Washington probably trails only Christianity on society's least wanted list. It's time to stand saints!

Again, Israel is not even getting an honorable mention these days on either side in the primaries. I think this is fall-out from the present administration, who probably thinks Israel is not very important today, even though it's the only democracy in the Middle East. As the biblical worldview dwindles in the United States and the secular worldview takes over, the biblical promises concerning those who bless Israel will be blessed of God will be forgotten. I recently saw a number of pastors at a gun range on the news qualifying with guns; supposedly for protection of whom?

On the evening news yesterday, it was reported that a man was breaking into a home; the owner shot him wounding him in the arm. The owner was charged for shooting him and now the thief has sued the owner for pain, suffering and hospital bills. Christ is still the answer!

Recently the "700 Club" news broadcast showed a situation happening in Indonesia, the largest Muslim nation in the world, a group called the Islamic Defenders Fund are violently attacking Christian churches to the point that the churches have all been closed down accept one that was allowed to operate due to a friendship between the pastor and a Muslim who intercedes for him and his Pentecostal Church. This group is so powerful, they persuade the local governments not to issue *permits* for Christian churches to operate (down from 69 churches to 1)!

I believe that on the horizon some where in this great country is a judge or some other influential person watching and waiting for the opportunity to pull this *permit business* on some local Christian churches. Will they win this time or the next, or the next, or the next? Only a heavenly intervention will save us – and that, only if the churches pray sincerely, repent and turn the people of God back to *His* New Testament "pattern" of believer-priests, *all* living sacrifices to the glory of God.

My wife and I suffered a home invasion a few years ago. I won't go into all the details; I assured the two men who both had pistols one my head and the other to my wife's head that we had no weapons in the house. The more vicious one of the two told me to get any weapons and all of the valuable together; he guarded me as we searched the house – he said things like "if I find a gun or any money or valuables that you have held back, my partner is going to blow your wife's brains out."

A while later, satisfied with their take, they locked us in a bathroom and made their escape. We got out and dialed 911. Then I saw it! My dad's 4/10 shotgun was against the wall less than a foot away behind the partially closed door of the very room where the threats were made. That gun was hidden in plain sight! After my father died, I had brought the gun home and put it there and totally had forgotten it. We thanked and praised God for keeping us safe through the whole ordeal.

"God kept my thoughts and the thief's eyes off the Gun!"

A couple of days after the media showed the pastors on the gun range, a notable Bible College president announced to the media and the world that he was going to allow guns on the campus. Though much of this makes all the sense in the world – it's still like trying to put out a fire with gasoline. I would rather just trust God and His Word!

A couple of years ago, on a James Roberson's "Life Today" broadcast, Pastor John Hagee told his testimony about a man standing eight feet out in front of the altar behind which he was standing and threatening that he was going to kill him. He fired six shots, when the police measured the paths of each of the bullets all of which were embedded in the wall behind him three passed on his left and the other three passed him on the right! Have faith in God!

Where are we to find help?

Help for America is where it has always been, from whence we've fallen. We must remember, repent, and return to God. We now have a generation coming to the forefront at all levels of society who have been taught through academia and our mighty media that there are no biblical absolutes. To them there is no absolute truth. Truth is up to the individual or so says humanity.

GOD ALWAYS HAS THE LAST WORD!

This deadly philosophy of no moral truth and truth is up to the individual has begun to invade the leadership of the Christian community. It is my prayer that God will raise-up a generation of people like Daniel and the three Hebrews; who filled with the Holy Spirit will stand to the glory of God on the truths of God's Word bursting with moral courage, no matter what!

"The God who made the world and everything in it is the Lord of heaven and earth and does not live in temples built by human hands. And He is not served by human hands, as if He needed anything. Rather, He Himself gives everyone life and breath and everything else" (Acts 17:24-25).

REFLECTION AND DISCUSSION QUESTIONS: CHAPTER 19

1. Whoever makes them self a friend of the world makes his or her _____ a _____ of God.

2. In the world sin is considered acceptable and pleasurable. Discuss the ramifications:

3. The world has lost its very _____ of sin.

4. The Book of Daniel emphasizes the _____ of God in the _____ of nations.

5. Holding to convictions will either _____ your _____ or _____.

6. I can apply this lesson to my life by:

7. Closing Statement of Commitment:

CHAPTER TWENTY

Tradition and Truth

"This people honor Me with their lips
but their heart is far from Me.
and in vain they worship Me,
teaching as doctrines the
commandments of men."
– (Mark 7:7)

Today the word tradition is like poison in a contemporary society to include some people in the church. Often you hear that it is outdated, boring, and other words to indicate a real problem with loss of the true definition. Many of Christianity's foundational words have suffered this same demise, a common occurrence today. The problem really is not tradition.

The Greek word for tradition is *paradosis* meaning "a handing down" to the next generation.[16] The problem is not tradition but *traditionalism*, which is the worship or idolizing of manmade traditions.

Thus, some manmade traditions become more precious to the people than the truths of God's Word. This prevents them being examined especially so much and so that few people dare to touch them or try to change them. In fact, many traditions become hindrances to spiritual growth when they are no longer useful as means to an end.

The problem occurs when instead of discarding the outdated traditions; the churches adopt them as ends in themselves. Annual calendars derived from the traditions of men have actually crowded out any thought of doing the church's biblical mission [of making disciples and teaching them] in many local churches across this nation.

This happens when a church becomes confused, spiritually cold, and unscriptural in their vision casting. Unless traditionalism is countered it will totally destroy the kingdom effectiveness of any local church. We are experiencing a rapid increase in the deterioration of marriage and the family, home, government, and all other foundational institutions as rejection of Christ, biblical truth and the Holy Spirit becomes the way of the land.

No matter what the secular philosophers, gurus and soothsayers have to offer, Christ is the Truth of God's Word and therefore He is the standard for our conduct and behavior. Attempting to deny the existence of Christ, who actually created it all and holds it all together is ludicrous; especially for those who claim to be His!

The authentic Church of the Living God is a supernatural community under King Jesus, who is the Head. This identity established at Pentecost and remaining unto this day is that His disciples are His hands and His feet, members of His body – reaching out to fallen humanity on errands of love, mercy, and compassion.

Acute hypocrisy

While Jesus ministered here on the earth, our Lord encountered Jewish traditions that were more important to them than their inspired Torah because traditionalism had replaced their religious tradition (see Mark 7:1-23). The Pharisees were upset with Jesus and His disciples because they ate food without going through the ceremonial washings; adding to their fury was Jesus' eating meals with tax collectors and sinners. Both acts were clearly in violation of the law.

Jesus began the argument with the Pharisees by calling them hypocrites. Hypocrite refers to [actors who wear different masks in theater as they play different characters]. Therefore, the Pharisees were not genuinely religious; they were simply playing a role before the people and obscuring authentic truth. This hypocrisy defines many Christians individually and corporately in the American Church today.

Traditionalism versus Innovation

Often someone will jokingly quote these supposedly seven last words of a dying church. "We have never done it like that!" This attitude can cripple or bring immediate death to innovation and relevance. It is not a joking matter! Many churches operating today has few millennials in their membership as a result. I remember in my childhood the officers calling the young people, the church of tomorrow. That was probably alright in those days – but they are part of the present church today; and many of them are spiritually and physically missing in action. They don't want to be mere spectators – so they break ranks with family traditions and move on to churches where they can be involved; and not waiting to grow old.

Today the millennials are neglected at home and church, [growing up without the foundational biblical teaching, moral training and absolute truth] so needed for proper spiritual growth. We wrestle with the tension of traditionalism and innovation in all Christian thought today. Because of traditionalism in its many shades many churches refuse to make any changes good or bad and that's worse. At the same time, many of the new churches springing up across this country would be almost unrecognizable to the generations of believers that have now passed off the scene; and now they are beginning to affect many seniors yet in the church today. Many of the churches have their own home-grown brand of spirituality.

However, if we spend too much time evaluating an innovation and its ripple effects it may have on society and our lives, the new blessed thing may well pass us by. The deep assurance that everything will be pretty much the same for the next ten years is not valid.

Powerful resistance

Two very powerful enemies have reared their heads and resist positive innovation in many local churches today, Pharisee (ism) and relativism. Throughout the history of the church you see that God has created innovation after innovation for His church.

Pharisee (ism)

Instead of blessing God's innovation today's Pharisees [un-anointed leaders] like those of old are opposed to any change from the status quo. They are powerful enough to get their way politically, and many times out-number the anointed leaders. Paul tells us that Satan will take advantage of us if we remain ignorant to his devices (see 2 Corinthians 2:11). So, let's not be ignorant of these devices:

- He explores our comfort zones and resists change.
- He explores our tendency to ignore the lessons of history.
- He explores our arrogant exclusivism.
- He explores our hesitancy to allow God to use our minds and emotions over reason.

- He explores our tendency not to self-evaluate our heritage.
- He explores our love of position and power.

Relativism

Just as the so-called free-spirit revolution of the 60's rose up and caught many churches unprepared for it – the evil of relativism is ravaging the church today. Relativism is the theory that there is no objective standard by which *truth* may be determined, so supposedly truth varies with individuals and circumstances. Again, we are haunted with a revolution "born and raised" in academia, which has reached critical mass in all areas of our society!

The claim of this revolution, [relativism] is that all truth is *subjective.* So, if all truth is subjective – then what we know as *"objective truth"* is dead. Though we know that relativism is not true, *it has been accepted as true.* Society at large has been arrested by contradictory situations. For example, suppose I say, "there is a spare tire in the trunk of the car" and you say, "there is a spare tire in the trunk of the car" – and we both are right, then there must be and not be a spare tire in the trunk of the car right now, at the same time. That is impossible!

Some argue that "if truth is relative, then no one is ever wrong – even when they are. If something is true to me, then I'm right even when I am wrong. But believe it or not the social engineers who prepare curriculums of local schools and institutions of higher learning have not skipped a beat at indoctrinating and reorienting our children and young millennials with this secular perspective based on relative truth [personal experiences]. This tragic philosophy plays out in attitudes and belief systems that say,

- If it feels good do it!
- Do your own thing.
- You choose your truth, and I'll choose mine.
- Hey, if it works for you it's okay.
- Who are you to judge me?

These phrases popularized in songs and heard all over the country today are signaling a shift in society from absolute truth to relative truth and from a biblical worldview to a secular worldview. Accordingly, truth in the world today is negotiable and can be freely altered to suit the person, the mood, or the situation as seen played out in the government, courts, education, media and other institutions across the land daily. That does not mean it's right.

Therefore, truth is different for different persons. You can do your own thing and I'll do mine. We won't bother judging each other about what is right and what is wrong; to do so would be totally intolerant (definition in the eyes or feelings of the beholder)! Pastors we've got to teach biblical and Spiritual truth, now! We must be obedient to the Lord's command (see Matthew 28:18-20).

American lifestyle

The condition of serving "me, myself, and I" makes it extremely difficult for us to take up our cross and deny self which is essential if we are going to fulfill God's pattern of walking in the power of the Holy Spirit – the only power that can develop the characteristics Jesus taught.

Walking in the old natural flesh is becoming the norm for many, because carnality has so displaced holiness in many churches. The sad results of this are made evident when we examine the fruits of our society and how little influence Christian standards now have on the way people live as compared to the influence of the world on the average Christian. How we carry ourselves while handling the everyday affairs of life is the true reflection of our Christian character [salt and light].

The hybrid has landed

Satan will use some Scripture if it will benefit him or suit his purposes; of course, it will always be twisted in his favor. It seems that tolerance is accepted in our culture today, but in a contradictory sense. Those people who cry for tolerance are themselves intolerant of the people they consider intolerant! What they are really saying is, *"agree with me and you won't be intolerant."* We see this played out daily in the media.

Our children, after being bombarded and taught daily from the secular perspective; when confronted in the churches with the teaching and preaching of absolutes deserves to be given a full explanation of the differences. We now have people clashing with both persuasions in every level of leadership in the land and that includes the church. Many who have been exposed to relativism through education and societal pressures – are not balanced with similar amounts of sound biblical truth.

In fact, many probably consider the inspired truth of God's Word that we preach and teach to be just our opinions. Whose report are you going to believe.

Absolute moral truth

Moral relativism is relativism applied to the morals of a society. First, what is a society?

- A voluntary association of persons for common ends.
- A part of a community bound together by common interests and standards.

To be sure, from this definition it is difficult to determine what the relevant society is. If a person from one society is cohabiting with a person from another society, and a person from a third society moves in next door that holds a different view than theirs; which society determines whether this living arrangement is right or wrong? The cohabiting couple is the relevant society for determining whether their living arrangement is right or wrong.

Moral relativism suffers from a problem known as reformer's dilemma, if moral relativism is true, then it is logically *impossible* for a society to have virtuous moral reformers, those of us who agree with and preach and teach the Word of God without compromise. Why?

- Moral reformers and true ministers are members of a society who stand outside that society's code and pronounce a need for reform and change in that code.
- However, if an act is right; and only if it is in keeping with a given society's code, then the reformer or minister is an immoral person – for his or her views are at odds with those of their society.

I think many of us fail to see the implications of what this could mean in reference to our pulpits and the truth of our convictions as God's messengers know that our "religious freedoms" are more threatened with each passing day. By their definition, we are always wrong because our convictions go against the code of secular society:

- A few years back the Mayor of Houston, Texas ordered copies of some of the city's more prominent pastor's weekly sermons to see if they were out of sync with present societal thoughts on homosexuality. It did not happen, but that was probably a trial run – Satan won't give up that easy.
- On December 31, 2015, the evening news carried the story of 190 Muslim factory workers being fired over a conflict of prayer time. The boss said no, and they went to prayer anyway. Religious freedom?

Some acts are wrong regardless of social convictions. Advocates of this idea usually adopt the standpoint of particularism and claim that all people can know some things are wrong, such as sexual abuse of children, rape, murder, stealing, and such without first needing criteria for knowing how it is that they do, in fact know such things.

Thus, an act of sexual abuse can be wrong and known to be wrong even if society says it is right, an act can be right and known to be right even if society says it is wrong. In fact, an act can be right or wrong even if society says nothing whatsoever about that act.

If normative relativism is true, there is nothing intrinsically right about the moral views in either of the societies represented above or any society for that matter. For this reason, moral relativism must be rejected!

What is truth?

Dr. Francis Schaffer called something that is always true, true truth. Whether people agree or disagree with it and whether it happens to be part of their experience. Absolute biblical truth and moral values remain absolute and are true, whether you agree with it. Many secular humanists and atheists have escalated their subtle strategies over the past sixty or more years to plant relativism throughout society mainly through secular public education, academia, the media and the school of public opinion. As a result society has lost the confidence that statements of fact can ever be anything more than opinions; we no longer know that anything is certain beyond our own subjective thoughts with the idea that the word truth now means relative "truth to me" or "truth to you."

Therefore, these ideas have very subtly taken root in all areas of society and are very difficult to remove. Every part of truth die including ethics and morality with it. A good example of this came several years ago in the "Afluenza" case. A young teenager received probation after causing an automobile accident which killed four people while driving under the influence of alcohol. The defense won the case by *inventing* a new word in his defense, *"affluenza"* meaning spoiled by riches! If truth cannot be known, then the concept of moral truth becomes blurred, *ethics* become relative, right and wrong become matters of individual opinion. Relativism is wrecking the peace in more and more homes and churches today! Certainly, we see its operation clearly in our Federal Government today. By the time the impeachment trial is over, we'll need a new edition of the legal dictionary. Truth is kicked under the bus today. God forbid! Many leaders are trying to deal with this through compromise. You can't change God's "pattern!" While there seem to be a lull today in these types of satanic tactics, pastors please know these types of incidents can resurface any day because "relativism" and its cousin the "new tolerance" are entrenched in this present generation as normal today. We are at the point that church leaders are going to have to stand and lead or get out of the way! God is able!

Perhaps the time is past in America when true Christians can standby the Word. Who took the word dogmatic out of our theological discussions? Brothers and sisters its time to be dogmatic about the Word of God. Who said, "we shouldn't defend the truth of God's Word?"

Morality's erosion

If there is no truth, nothing has transcendent value, including human beings. The death of morality reduces people to the status of mere animals:

- When people are viewed as things, they begin to be treated as things.
- We are witnessing a generation that has institutionalized moral relativism. Their most subtle goal is to be happy and that justifies using any means to reach that end.
- If society rejects spiritual moral truth, why should we be surprised as we see the daily encroachment of evil and the increasing downward spiral of moral turbulence?

We are seeing and experiencing the results of this philosophical lie daily as murder, mayhem and moral degradation skyrocket downward. Once these ideas took root and became the new norm, people began to resign themselves to believe the old post-Christian adage, "that's just the way it is!"

Unchanging reality

The unchanging reality for the Christian is the Word of God; this is the standard for absolute truth. God tells us He is the same yesterday, today, and forever, so we know that His truth cannot be altered simply because we might disagree with it.

Do you believe that God's absolute truth is just as unchanging when it comes to the sins of the flesh in Galatians 5:19-21? The Scripture says, "The works of the flesh are evident, which are:

- Adultery – unlawful sexual relations outside of marriage (Galatians 5:19; Matthew 5:32; 15:19).
- Fornication – all manner of other unlawful relations (Matthew 5:32).
- Uncleanness – all forms of sexual perversion (v. 16; Romans 1:21-32; 6:19).
- Lewdness – anything tending to promote sexual sin (v. 19; 2 Peter 2:7).
- Idolatry – passionate affections upon things (v. 2; Colossians 3:5).
- Witchcraft – practice of dealing with evil spirits (v. 20; Revelation 22:15).
- Hatred – bitter dislike; abhorrence (v. 20; Ephesians 2:15-16).
- Variance – discord, dissensions, quarreling (v. 2; Romans 1:29).
- Emulations – jealousies, envies, outdo others, zeal (v. 20; Romans 10:2).
- Outburst of wrath – indignation, fierceness (v. 20; Ephesians 4:31; Colossians 3:8).
- Dissensions – disorder, parties, divisions (v. 20; 1 Corinthians 3:3).
- Heresies – goes astray from truth (v. 20; Acts 5:17; Galatians 2).
- Envy – jealous of others' blessings (v. 21; Matthew 27:18).
- Murders – to kill, hatred (v. 21; 1 John 3:15).
- Drunkenness – living intoxicated (v. 21; Romans 13:13).
- Revelries – rioting, sinful activities (v. 21; 1 Peter 4:3; Romans 13:13).
- And the like

This passage of Scripture ends with, "those who practice such things will not inherit the kingdom of God. Although believers can commit these sins, those people whose character is summed up in uninterrupted and unrepentant practice of then cannot belong to God. Therefore, they are not permitted to enter the spiritual kingdom of redeemed people over whom Christ now rules (see Ephesians 5:5).

After more than forty years of observing the church close up in various positions of leadership, I think it is safe to say that as we view the behaviors above, many people in the Christian community no longer view them as absolutely right or wrong, but relative.

It is so sad the way some denominations are changing their constitutions and by-laws to enable them to accommodate these sins of the flesh and sinners as normal. The Scriptures distinctly state, the only way to overcome these fleshly sins is repent of all sin and live in the power of the Holy Spirit as He works through our spirit (see Galatians 5:25).

Where such behavior, it is positive proof that the persons are not in reality living in the power of the Holy Spirit (see Galatians 5:16, 18, 22, 23), but are being energized by Satan and his host of demons (see Matthew 16:23; Acts 5:3).

Paul repeatedly encourages believers to overcome the sins of the flesh by living in the Spirit. As stated in an earlier section, "the unbeliever can live only in the flesh – but the believers can live in the flesh or in the Spirit, but not at the same time."

Deliverance ministry and church discipline must be reintroduced taught and practiced in the Christian church.

Walking in Spirit and in Truth [reality]

When we face reality, it is apparent that our best human efforts are founded upon limited human faculties and the best estimates we can make of any situation are flawed and lacking. God's pattern and calling upon those who are His are based upon His perfect understanding of fundamental and ultimate reality. That is the glory of walking in the Spirit and biblical truth, notice:

- It sets forth things as they really are.

- The true Christian's diagnosis of all the world's ills from conflicts between nations to conflicts with worldviews and cultures, to conflicts in the individual's soul is accurate because it reflects a true understanding of the human condition.
- The New Testament Epistles always begins with the truth [doctrine]. The writers there always call us back to reality. Then based on that underlying *foundation of the truth of God's Word*, they go on to offer certain practical applications. Why start with anything less than truth?

In the first three chapters of the Book of Ephesians, Paul establishes several clear purpose statements for the people of God, not just for eternity, but for the increasingly perilous times in which we live today:

1. The church is to reflect the holiness of God (Ephesians 1:14).

- God chose us before the foundation of the world.
- That we should be holy and blameless in love.
- His plan and strategy are obviously independent of human influence [according to *His* pattern].
- His people are to be moral examples to the world, reflecting the pure character and holiness of Jesus Christ, who resides within us.

2. The church is to reveal God's glory (v.5).

- The first purpose of the church is not the welfare of humanity, though their welfare is important to God. Multitudes were moved while the media *praised* Pope Francis during his visit here several years ago, for his attention to the welfare of humanity.
- The first purpose God chose for each of us to live to the praise and glory of God, so that through our lives His glory will be revealed to the world. The New English Bible states it, "We should cause His glory to be praised." "Make God look good!"

3. The church is to be a witness to Christ (1 Peter 2:9).

- The apostle Peter offers concerning the church's witnessing role, "You are a chosen race, a royal priesthood, a holy nation, God's own people, that you may declare the wonderful deeds of Him who called you out of darkness into the marvelous light."

We are indwelt by Christ so that He may demonstrate His life and character through us. The responsibility to fulfill this calling of the church belongs to every true New Testament believer-priest. The expression of the church's witness may sometimes be corporate, but the responsibility to witness to Christ is always individual.

It is always easy for the church or the individual Christian to talk about displaying the character of Christ; however, upon close observation the image many Christians display is not the true biblical image of Jesus Christ. Therefore, in Ephesians 4:2-3, Paul describes the biblical marks of Christlike character:

- Love
- Humility
- Patience
- Unity
- Peace

The Spirit-bestowed oneness of all true N.T. believer-priests has created the bond of peace, the spiritual cord that surrounds and binds God's holy people together. That bond is love (see Colossians 3:14).

The church must wait on the Lord, be patient and forbearing knowing that the truths of God's Word take time to sprout and grow, and time to produce a harvest.

The Spirit-filled Church of the Living God is not to demand that society make abrupt changes to long established social patterns. Rather the church is to promote positive social change by shunning evil and *living righteously*, "according to pattern" – then the truth of God's Word will take root in society and bear the fruit of change.

REFLECTIONS AND DISCUSSION QUESTIONS: CHAPTER 20

1. What is the significance of "speaking into the life" of the next generation?

2. Instead of discarding obsolete traditions, many churches make them _____.

3. The Church of the Living God is a _____ community under _____ _____, the Head.

4. His _____ are His hands and His feet reaching out to a _____ World.

5. Briefly discuss in the space below Tradition versus Innovation as they are referred to in this chapter:

6. I can apply this lesson to my life by:

7. Closing Statement of Comment:

SECTION IX

Contend for the Faith

CHAPTER TWENTY-ONE

Contend for the Faith

"Beloved, while I was very diligent to write to you concerning our common salvation, I found it necessary to write to you exhorting you to contend earnestly for the faith which was once for all delivered to the saints." Emphasis added.
– Jude 3

I can recall as a young boy listening to the old saints testify in Wednesday night prayer meeting. We watched and learned much from them. They always began their testimony with a hope and determination [heaven!]. They did not live as if God owed them something, everyday with its troubles and circumstances was a day that the Lord had made and no matter what, they would rejoice and be glad in it. I can still hear their echo, "If it's the Lord's will!"

Vertical Living

Those saints lived God-centered lives in a right relationship with Him and others. Being a pastor's kid, I had the opportunity to witness several deaths of saints in their homes in those days [tagging along and sometimes being dragged along]. Our father taught us that dying was a part of living. I even witnessed a couple of people as they drew their last breath; it was peaceful, [with the true saints], then at the funeral some saint would exclaim, "Didn't she have a nice smile on her face?" I'd look in the casket and sure enough, a smile! These were real saints of God looking forward to joining their true fellow Christian friends and loved ones "some glad morning when this life is over, and they would fly away – to that land on God's celestial shores!"

Horizontal Living

Many of today's funerals [also called a celebration of life by some] consist mostly of hearing family members and friends speak of their favorite encounters with the deceased during his or her lifetime. You hear comments like "he made me laugh" or "she's an angel now" or "he or she is up there looking down on us." In today's America the destination of the deceased is more closely guarded [relatively speaking?], so the best way even for some preachers seems to be to follow along or just leave that [life] alone, rather than to make it clear. Therefore, it is left up to Hollywood's idea such as the old "Touched by an Angel" deception repeatedly.

Today the so-called progressive Christians are trying to substitute the Christian faith in many local churches with an earthly horizontally focused pseudo-religious Christianity based on Jesus' earthly walk in Galilee. Each aspect can easily be adjusted to their worldly wishes; based on the Lord's love for all people reflected in His inclusivity, for example. However, these same horizontal folks fail to speak of His virgin birth, sinless life, death and glorious resurrection and ascension [foundational doctrine]. The verticals address sin and righteous living – and the purpose of His coming.

This horizontal [cultural] mode of living has invaded the Christian church and many church leaders are shocked to find out that these people have a different agenda. Their agenda reared its head during the court decision on same-sex marriages; as church leaders scrambled to change constitutions and by-laws in order to accommodate the laws of the land; which in fact violates God's moral law. During the present administration, their media activity seems to be curtailed in forward movement of their progressive agenda. The progressives have moved to action. Everywhere active homosexuals and lesbians are in the forefront. Even in the run for the presidency? Beware, as the old saying goes, "there's always a lull before the storm." What has happened to "We the people?" It's God's moral law at stake, not man's law!

This is an apostate position [compromise] which will never be accepted in heaven!

When the vertical brethren stand up for God's Moral Law, we are called intolerant, bigoted, etc.by the horizontal folk. Defend the faith!

Pastors be warned the next political attempt by the progressives will probably be to give equal rights [to any office in the church] to live in sin at the same time legalize their demand full membership in your church. Some might think that is already happening, and perhaps that's true in some churches. Even the unsaved realize that is not the norm. Once the horizontals get the civil law passed, if the verticals are not careful and begin to only become more passive refusing to even join the conversation or anything else – the horizontals [culture] win simply by forfeiture.

Barna research reflected a survey of more than a thousand pastors asked if they ever mention such current issues of the day from the pulpit or discussed them with their congregations, only five percent said they did. Ninety-five percent said they never discuss such issues. That attitude is very devastating, especially for black congregations. As a pastor and Bible teacher I cannot see how we can be relevant in our delivery if we are silent on the controversial issues. Pastors aren't we supposed to interpret the times? Preachers don't let anyone dismiss you from the conversation!

Worldly people are very creative in this feeling oriented society, and to many, it is not uncommon for them to strive to blend the Worship service, funerals or wedding by introducing their own vows or words, rituals, music, and even the eulogy with their personal unscriptural comments as a substitute for the sermon and many times deny our Lord Jesus Christ with the pastor's blessing. This ought to not be! We are to always be reminded, "according to pattern." Often-time pastors and some other church leaders assimilate their fears rather than confront them.

Contend for the Faith

Much of the body of Christ is in jeopardy today because many carnally minded churches, feel more comfortable acting like Cain. They would rather have a pseudo-religious Christianity and refuse to accept the true faith that requires a repentance, a new birth, and a righteous life. Additionally, failure to equip of the membership cripples them in any attempt to participate in the work of spiritual and biblical ministry. Hiring professionals to do the work leaves the membership as mere un-deployed spectators.

I was mainly an equipper during my thirty years as pastor. My philosophy of ministry was to spiritually and biblically base train and equip *all* subordinate leaders in the priesthood of all believers, who in turn train *all* of their members as believer-priests in their areas of influence and responsibility. The ministry of all believers is the 2 Timothy 2:2, model of ministry. Though it is not easy – employing active "spirit and truth" small group ministry is essential in a "counter to the culture" with this model.

The church is not fully the church of God if she is not fully engaged through the Holy Spirit to ensure that *all the members* receive essential biblical doctrine and training in the mission [inside] work of edification (developing the fruit and spiritual gifts for building up the body) and [outside] work of witness-evangelism (every believer-priest applying to their own life and presenting to the world, the gospel message of salvation and the kingdom). The world attempts to convince Christians to adapt to their concept of tolerance and privacy by keeping their views, beliefs, and practices within the church's four-walls!

Christ left explicit instructions for the Church (all the church), but for the past five or six decades; much of the body has moved so far away from *His will*. What He requires of His body is now considered obsolete by a great portion of today's church. One day Jesus was asked to identify the most important command. His response put all the Old Testament [all the Law and the Prophets] in a nutshell two objectives:

(1) The Great Commandment

> *"Love the Lord your God with all your heart and with all your soul and with all your mind....... Love your neighbor as yourself. All the Law and the Prophets hang on these two commandments"* (Matthew 22:37-40).

Later in some of His final remarks to His disciples, Jesus gave them the Great Commission which assigned *three* more objectives: Go make disciples, baptize them, and teach them to obey everything He had taught them.

(2) The Great Commission

> *"Go and make disciples of all nations, baptizing them in the name of the Father and of the Son and of the Holy Spirit, and teaching them to obey everything I have commanded you"* (Matthew 28:19-20). Emphasis added.

In these two great admonitions of Christ to His people, He reveals five-pointed evangelism mission of His will for every local church to accomplish. Therefore, the mission of all Christian Communities should be centered around these five ministries to be authentic. The commission of evangelism *is* so important; Christ expressed it in five sub-commissions one in each of the four gospels and one in the book of Acts, carefully study each of the five scriptural applications below:

- Matthew 28:19-20
- Mark 16:17
- Luke 24:47-49
- John 20:21
- Acts 1:8

Christ commissions every truly born-again believer to go and tell the world the message of salvation. God has called and invited us to be a part of His eternal pattern to bring people into His family. We have backing us, the power of the gospel, [the Holy Spirit and Word], to whom we yield ourselves as instruments to be used for God's glory. In accomplishing the commission, we are fulfilling the kingdom mission of the church we go:

- We "make disciples"
- We "baptize them"
- We "teach them to obey [all]"
- We "send them into the Lord's service"

In spite of what (they), the "fleshly" or "carnally-minded" part of the local church have to say about it, (we) the true "spiritual" children of God know that as long as there is one person in the world who does not know Jesus Christ, the church is mandated [by Christ] to continue the kingdom mission. God wants people saved! If the kingdom of God and the will of God is not our first priority, then we have failed to obey Him. Jesus admonished us to:

> *"Seek first the kingdom of God and His righteousness, and all these things shall be added to you"* (see Matthew 6:33).

We must understand individually and corporately that partial obedience is disobedience. We have our marching orders to do until He returns for us. A command is not a suggestion or recommendation; it is an order and, in this case, to be carried out not by our will – but His will as stated scripturally.

We the People

People must be able to see how they fit into the accomplishment of the Church's kingdom mission. When the mission is clearly stated and understood everyone can not only believe in it, but they can participate in the successful meeting and accomplishing of all stated goals and objectives. Again, we must encourage the participation of every believer, this is crucial.

The believer's "need" to belong and to serve is not satisfied in the model where the ministry task is left to the pastor and it never gets done because the ministry task is simply too great. The membership must be equipped to reach the lost and to minister to the spiritual needs of a world spiraling downward under the weight of growing evil worldwide in these perilous times.

A major hindrance to "…..... the unity of the faith and the knowledge of the Son of God …" (see Ephesians 4:14) is the fact that many churches and Christians are divorcing themselves from the Holy Spirit [the Spirit of truth] and [the blood of Jesus]; therefore they lean to reason and their own understanding [the flesh]. If believer-priests are to be equipped, the church leadership must realize that:

- They must be born again.
- They must be delivered of all access baggage [flesh].
- They must be Spirit-filled.
- They must realize their own brokenness and total dependence on the Lord.
- They must understand that no one knows it all.
- They must have a teachable spirit.
- Each believer-priest needs a Spirit-filled mentor for accountability as they contend for the faith.

The Spirit-filled equippers are given to us to keep us from being tossed to and fro; and carried about by every wind of false doctrine and false teaching.

REFLECTION AND DISCUSSION QUESTIONS: CHAPTER 21

1. Discuss the meaning and importance of passing on the doctrine the incarnation of Jesus Christ to the next generation.

2. Discuss the pastors' responsibility to talk about current events with the congregation.

3. Explain below what is meant by "Cain's religion.

4. What are the two elements of the Great Commandment?

5. Briefly explain the four elements of the Great Commission in Matthew 28:19:
   1.
   2.
   3.
   4.

6. I can apply this lesson to my life by:

7. Closing Statement of Commitment:

CHAPTER TWENTY-TWO

A Subtle Substitute

*"For certain men have crept in unnoticed, who long ago were marked
out for this condemnation, ungodly men, who turn the grace of God into
lewdness and deny the only Lord God and our Lord Jesus Christ."*
– Jude 4

The peril which confronted Jude and his fellow believers was the existence and power of false teachers infiltrating the church two thousand years ago. Jude illustrates the fact that the most subtle and alarming attacks upon Christianity have been made by those within the church.

They were pretending to be the true, they looked like the real thing, but their intentions from the very beginning were to lead God's people away from the true faith through contamination. Their goal has not changed over the centuries and to this day it continues to make salvation by grace an occasion for licentiousness and regard the gospel of Christ as simple "foolishness," thereby denying the only Lord God, and our Lord Jesus Christ [see Romans 1:25].

Two thousand years ago, Jude discerned Satan's tactic of planting his counterfeits among the true saints, with the intention of destroying the true Christianity. His demonic agents employ his deceptions through counterfeit theories and beliefs, such as humanism, hedonism, multiculturalism, relativism; and bogus pseudo-religions to confuse and hide the true revelation truth of God's Word from God's people. He is employing that same tactic today in the American church while enjoying an increasing amount of success as fewer Christians each year search the Scriptures for truth. The benefits of the Holy Spirit's ministry are critically denied in many of our churches due to the churches' adoption of secular leadership styles, organizational practices, spiritual and biblical illiteracy and successful earthly forms that deny the power [Holy Spirit] are promoted today.

Jude sees these enemies of the faith entrenched; and sounds the trumpet of danger; he calls on the saints in every generation to wage a vigorous battle to preserve the most holy faith and the deeper things of God (vv. 3, 2). Pastors, deacons, stewards, and other leaders of the local churches must realize that their first duty is to love God and keep the church doctrinally [truth] pure.

Jude characterized false teachers:

- They are ungodly.
- They pervert grace.
- They deny Christ.

Can I get a witness?

Concerning these false teachers, the apostle Peter said, "These are wells without water, clouds carried by a tempest, for whom is reserved the blackness of darkness forever" (2 Peter 2:17).

- A well without water would be very disappointing in a hot desert climate. So are false teachers who pretend to have spiritual water to quench thirsty souls; but they produce nothing.
- The coming clouds would seem to promise rain, but the storm moved around leaving the land dry. Likewise, the false teachers might seem to promise spiritual refreshment, but were all show with no substance.

Yes – we will stand!

How are Christians to act considering the growing apostasy and the growing menace of false teachers? The growth of apostasy is more evidence of Satan's hatred and determination to block the truth of God's Word. I might add here, he has been increasingly successful in recent years. To counter this situation the believer-priests are to remember the Word and the Spirit work together (see 2 Peter 3).

Believers are to grow spiritually through the Word. Therefore, when Jude points out that those false teachers are **without the Spirit,** he leaves no doubt as to their eternal destiny. They are simply worldly people who do not belong to God. Emphasis added.

Notice Jude doesn't believe that intellectual arguments are the best defense of the gospel. While he counters with the gospel of Jesus Christ, and the essentials of the "faith," he insists that the best argument against a paganized or secularized Christianity is a holy life built up in the most holy faith. He does not believe in going to the law and courts, nor is he pleading for their excommunication.

The seven-fold duty of the true Christians

Jude admonishes true Christians to:

- Build yourselves up in the most holy faith (see v. 20; 1 Timothy 1:4).
- Pray in the Spirit (see v. 20; Ephesians 6:18; Romans 8:26).
- Keep yourselves in the love of God (see v.21; 2 Timothy 1:14; Romans 8:35-39).
- Look for the mercy of our Lord and Savior, Jesus Christ (see v. 21; Hebrews 12:15).
- Have compassion on some, making a difference between those who are weak, spiritually and biblically weak and those who are proud and arrogant of heart and unwilling to obey truth (see v. 22).
- Save the willing with fear pulling them out of the fire of eternal hell (see v. 23).
- Hate even the garment spotted by the flesh (see v. 23; James 1:27; Ephesians 5:27).

Above all, believer-priests must be mature, prayerful, God-fearing, teachable and free from indwelling sin. Jude closes with a beautiful benediction emphasizing the power of God to:

1. Keep you from falling (v. 24; 1 Corinthians 10:13).
2. And present you faultless before the presence of His glory (see v. 24; Ephesians 5:27; Hebrews 7:25).

Free from indwelling sin

Earlier I pointed out that Paul stated clearly, the problem that causes the individual to be tossed to and fro is the flesh guided by the five senses (mind). This carnal [mind] condition is prevalent in many local churches today. In fact, to some it is considered normal. There is deliverance through Christ Jesus who delivers us from this body of death (sinful nature also called the old man). Paul cuts right to the solution – namely salvation is found *only* in Jesus Christ (see Romans 7:25).

In contrast he points to the freedom from indwelling sin, as the believer lives in the Spirit. We are empowered by the Spirit to live for Christ. The Scripture assures us in (Romans 8:1-2)

"There is therefore now no condemnation to those who are in Christ Jesus, who do not walk according to the flesh, but according to the Spirit. for the law of the Spirit of life in Christ Jesus has made me free from the law of sin and death."

We find a profile of the believer-priest who is free from indwelling sin in Galatians 5:22, 23 as he or she:

- Is "born from above" otherwise seeing and understanding the kingdom of God is impossible (see John 3:3).
- Is a living sacrifice (Romans 12:1).
- Is not conformed by the world; which causes the individual to see the Word through their circumstances; but he or she through a renewed mind see circumstances through the Spirit and the Word of God (see Romans 12:1, 2).
- Is wrapped in the righteousness of Jesus Christ (2 Corinthians 5:21).
- Is a new creation, all things are become new including a new divine human nature and God-centered spirit (see 2 Corinthians 5:17).
- Has put on the new man who has a renewed mind according to the image of Christ (Colossians 2:9-10).
- Has their needs met through the Spirit and their knowledge of God (see 1 Peter 1:3-4).
- Has the Spirit of Christ in his or her heart (see Galatians 4:6).
- Is joined to the Lord and is one spirit with Him (see 1 Corinthians 6:17).
- Has an anointing from the Holy One and knows all things (see 1 John 2:2).
- Has the power of Christ (see Ephesians 1:18-19).
- Has the mind of Christ (see 1 Corinthians 2:16).

This is possible only through our blood-washed spirit, new nature, and renewed soul and body that "according to pattern" are now complete in Christ!

The Christian's Character [bears repeating]

God went to great lengths to get Christians to walk in the Spirit; yet many are carnally minded and finding themselves trapped in conformity with the world's secular worldview. The major reason for this shortfall happens because the person does not seek the revelation knowledge of God's Word through the guidance and ministry of the Spirit of Truth.

Divine power and knowledge of God

There are unique expressions in the New Testament of divine power and knowledge of God. The Apostle Peter says,

> *"Grace and peace be multiplied to you in the knowledge of God and of Jesus our Lord, as His divine power has given to us all things that pertain to life and godliness, through the knowledge of Him who called us by glory and virtue, by which have been given to us exceeding and precious promises, that through these you may be partakers of the divine nature, having escaped the corruption that is in the world through lust"* (see II Peter 1:1-3; 1 Peter 1:18-21).

The Scripture warns that God's people perish for a lack of knowledge of God. We must remember the Word and the Spirit work together. The Scripture promises that walking in the Spirit through faith in the truth of God's Word; you shall not fulfill the lusts of the flesh (see Galatians 5:16). That is God's way out for His children during these perilous times; we must act upon the words of Jude 3 and contend for the faith once delivered to the saints. The evidence or fruit of our walk will manifest as the Spirit can develop them within us [the Christ character trait, love] listed in (vv. 22-23).

Paul used the singular word *fruit,* centering on the unifying love of Christ. Thus, each section of the nine-fold fruit of the Spirit is simply love in another revelation of the character of God through Christ and reflected to the world through the true believers-priests, who are "in Christ."

Paul warned that without the fruit of love no person could enter the kingdom of God. When most Christians think of the fruit of love, they usually think in terms cultivating and developing love relationships toward their brothers and sisters in Christ. However, it is not all that is involved in love.

There is another more important aspect of the fruit of love. Many Christians do not seem to realize that the Great Commandment is not, "Love one another." According to the Lord Himself in Matthew 22:37-39, a believer can love the brethren properly only *after first loving God:*

Jesus said unto him, *you shall love the Lord your God with all your heart, and with all your soul, and with all your mind. This is the first and great commandment. And the second is like the first; you shall love your neighbor as yourself.*

Some Christians are more comfortable with and express more love to others in the Body of Christ than they express to God. This is truly unbelievable! Their Father who loves them to the extent that He gave His only begotten Son to die for them (see John 3:16).

God desires that His children *know Him* to the extent that they are as comfortable in expressing love to Him publically as they are in their closet, this is the most intimate relationship on earth. Only then will the children of God come to know the Father in the Spirit as well as they know the people dearest to them in the flesh. It is imperative to know that knowing the Father to this extent on earth will be the *only* source of:

- Our confidence when we stand before the Son of God on that day that is yet to come (see John 14:8, 9).
- Many people today rely on expressing their love to the Father *indirectly* through doing good works. In that day when they stand before Him, *they will be rejected by Him.*

Jesus said in Matthew 7:22: *Many will say to me in that day, Lord, Lord have not we prophesied in your name? And in your name cast out demons? And in your name done many wonderful works?*

According to Jesus, one basis of His rejection of such people in that day will be expressed in the words – *I never knew you ....* (v. 23). Without these godly character qualities, the Christian's life cannot properly glorify God in the Spiritual gifts. Contend for the fruit!

It's very important that we come to realize that in our own strength, we cannot develop the fruit of love. Like the gifts of the Spirit, the Holy Spirit is cultivating and developing the fruit of love in us and it behooves us as true New Testament-believer priests to submit fully to Him and His ministry. The Greek word for *knew* is "ginosko" which means:

- To know by experience or effort

- To gain knowledge as the result of prolonged practice
- To get to know

Jesus was saying: "I never got to know you, for you did not cultivate that fruit of love and develop an intimate, loving relationship with Me." Therefore, we will greatly benefit in that day if we if we begin to develop a love relationship with the Father by cultivating this life-important fruit of love today, which will determine our eternal destiny. In addition to our future blessings, there are two present-day benefits for those who spiritually develop the fruit of love toward the Father:

The first benefit

The Father knew of the increasing danger of the cancerous fear all around us in society today. In Luke 21:26 Jesus Himself forewarned of the *fear* which was yet to come in our day:

> *"Men's hearts failing them from fear and the expectation of those things which are coming on the earth, for the powers of the heavens will be shaken."*

Many people today are dying of heart attacks in fulfillment of Jesus' prophecy that heart failure would be one of the indications and direct results of fear. The world is fast approaching a time when fear of Satan and evil circumstances will grip the hearts of men, women, boys, and girls to a greater degree than ever before:

- Fear of the unstable economic system.
- Fear of the ungodly world system in general can be seen globally gripping the hearts of men and women.
- Fear of the political and militaristic Middle East.
- Fear of international and home-grown terrorism.
- Fear of potential ethnic and racial misunderstanding which has elevated to pure hatred and voluntary segregation in many cases.
- Fear of inexperienced and ungodly judges, public and governmental leadership who are capable of worldly wisdom at best. Certainly, this is apparently seen today in many of the shallow decisions, laws and even the conversations of leadership at all levels.
- Fear of wild weather.

It is imperative that believers combat fear with love because fear will lead to many unhealthy actions in our lives. Fear is the root of much of the turmoil manifested in individuals in the church today. In general, many church people as well as unsaved people's sickness, oppression, and even death can be traced back to fear. Not only did Jesus warn His followers of the fear to come, but He also encouraged and presented them with an image of the Father that would cast out fear and cultivate His perfect love in our hearts:

> *"Are not two sparrows sold for a copper coin? And not one of them falls to the ground apart from your Father's will. But the very hairs of your head are all numbered. Do not fear; therefore, you are of more value than many sparrows."* Emphasis added.

The word therefore in v. 31 references the two previous verses. Jesus was making it clear to His disciples:

- When a sparrow falls to the ground, the Father knows about it.
- What Jesus was saying to His disciples then and [us today] was that if they would develop a relationship with God to the point of fully realizing their loving Father's awareness of each of them; they nor us would no longer fear. This kind of awareness comes only through cultivation.

Many believers in the local churches are not cultivating that love or coming to the knowledge of the truth.

The second benefit

The second benefit of developing the fruit of love toward the Father is that we are now enabled to conquer all things. Certainly, this means that God can never fail (see 1 Corinthians 13:8; 1 John 4:8).

The more we develop our love for God – the less we will fail in our individual lives, for we will know Him, the Mighty Conqueror. Then we can say with Paul, "What shall we say then to these things? "If God is for us then, who can be against us?" (Romans 8:31)

Aware of the Father as the Conqueror increases our confidence in His willingness and His ability to make us conquerors in our lives. *"God is for me."* Oh, what assurance!

There are many Christians today who cannot honestly identify with this claim from their hearts. When temptations come, they feel all alone – simply because they have not developed an individual love relationship with the Father. However, once one has developed that relationship, they can confidently shout with Paul, "Since God is with me, who can be against me?"

Without the knowledge of the truth, many Christians quote the familiar promise when the enemy is working in their lives – not realizing this promise is conditional to "them that love God." The more you love God, the more you will conquer trials and the more things will work together for your good.

Despite the false teachers, heresies, and religious forms of Christianity, satanic lies are released among those who profess, but do not possess the truth concerning the Spirit of love. You don't have to be deceived by false teachers! God is our Source and He has given us the Spirit of truth and His Word. So "be filled with the Spirit" (Ephesians 5:18) and study to show yourself approved unto God! The psalmist admonishes,

> *"How can a young man [or woman]*
> *keep his [or her] way pure?*
> *By living*
> *according to your word."*
> *--- Psalm 119:9 LASB*

America is drowning in a sea of impurity. Everywhere we look temptation to lead impure lives is present. In the Scripture above, the psalmist asked a question that troubles us all: how do we stay pure in such a filthy environment?

Jude's answer is that you maintain your life with God because:

- The Father has a personal interest in the preservation of those who belong to Christ.
- We are kept in Christ by the Holy Spirit.

How are New Testament believer-priests to act?

There is no better security possible than to be kept "in Christ." True believer-priests have a sure foundation provided in the teachings of the apostles and prophets. Believers are responsible to be obedient and faithful by living out their salvation, while God works out His will in and through them. However, we must vigorously put forth our sincere support in re-establishing Christian theology and reinforce emphasis in ministries and among denominations. People are seeking the answers to the big questions!

Jude warns us that, as we seek to help others, we must take care not to be defiled by them ourselves! As New Testament believer-priests, Christians must keep themselves unspotted from the world (see James 1:27).

In verse 1 we are saved: Additionally, we are to remain in the place of obedience where Christ's love is poured out on those who are His (see Philippians 2:12, 13; Romans 5:5).

As you read this epistle, it becomes evident that believer-priests must defend the faith and oppose false teachers wherever they are found. Christ is guarding us!

The deposit in us [truth]

As Christ guards and stands by us, likewise He wants us to guard the deposit He has left in our hands. Numerous Scriptures elaborate on this deposit which is the divine revelation of God's [truth] and how we are to guard and protect it in the local churches. I believe this is the major priority for pastors and deacons today. What Satan can't destroy; he will attempt at every opportunity to contaminate. Correct doctrine (truth) is best guarded as it becomes a part of our very being, our very lives. Again, Francis of Assisi spoke on this very crucial life, in 1225 A.D. when he said, "Preach, preach, and sometimes use words!" In 2 Timothy, the apostle Paul lays out the path for true New Testament believer-priests in the days of apostasy:

1. Faith (1:5)
2. The Holy Spirit (1:6, 7)
3. The Word of God (1:13; 3:1-17; 4:3, 4)
4. The grace of God (2:1)
5. Separation from vessels of dishonor (2:4, 20, 21)
6. The Lord's sure reward (4:7, 8)
7. The Lord's faithfulness and power (2:13, 19)

He calls these last days perilous times (3:1) and as we continue to read through the chapter, the apostasy or falling away is an *act of professed Christians who deliberately reject revealed truth.* For example:

- The deity of Jesus Christ
- Our redemption through Christ's atoning and redeeming sacrifice

Study carefully, 1John 3:16; 4:1-3; Philippians 3:18; 2 Peter 2:1 for a thorough understanding of these truths. I believe true righteous living Spirit-filled believer-priests, corporately is Christ's first line of defense:

- Against apostasy
- And the church's main responsibility "in the Spirit" is to "watch," "guard" and proclaim the "revealed truths of Scripture."

In 1Timothy 6:20, 21 Paul admonished Timothy and [the true church] through the prophesied future of the visible church's *apostasy* (see Luke 18:8; 2 Timothy 3:1-8) and the glory of the true Church manifested in the local churches (see Matthew 13:36-43; Romans 8:18-23; 1 Thessalonians 4:14-17). Listen:

"O Timothy!
Guard what was committed
to your trust
avoiding profane and idle babblings
and contradictions of what
is falsely called knowledge— by
some professing it
some have strayed concerning the faith.

False doctrine

What is falsely called knowledge [false doctrine] anything claiming to be the truth that is in fact a lie. For example, false teachers claim to have superior knowledge, but are ignorant in their understanding (see Colossians 2:8).

Words can hardly be found to describe the awful judgment awaiting those who reject Christ and teach Satan's lies. Some we might be able to save; but others may have gone too far, and we can only pity them. May God help us to be faithful and patiently await His coming!

Grace to you

Paul closes with the salutation "Grace to you" which is plural, and it goes far beyond Timothy to the whole congregation at Ephesus. All require the grace of God, especially if he or she is in ministry, and has the sacred trust to guard the revelation of God! (see 1 Corinthians 4:1; 1 Thessalonians 2:3, 4).

REFLECTIONS AND DISCISSION QUESTIONS: CHAPTER 22

1. What was happening in the church that warranted Jude's warning?

2. Discuss what characteristics did Jude mention identifies false teachers?

3. Discuss what happens to the church when the work of ministry is done by the pastor?

4. Discuss Jude's counter to paganism and secular Christianity?

5. Christians must be mature _____, God honoring, and _____ _____.

6. I can apply this lesson to my life by:

7. Closing Statement of Commitment:

CHAPTER TWENTY-THREE

You Shall be My Witness

*"But you shall receive power when the Holy Spirit has come
upon you; and you shall be witnesses to Me in Jerusalem, and
in Judea, and Samaria, and to the end of the earth"*
(Acts 1:8). Emphasis added.

One day traveling across Florida my wife and I saw a sign at a little motel that read, "Pets welcome – no children." As I pondered that I considered the fact that humanism is subtly making inroads with many people today; in this case, perhaps to them animals and people are on the same level – since to them both are animals or so says the evolutionists. Therefore, I'm sure the reasoning is that pets are a better choice than children, when all things are considered. God forbid!

A professor of a local university here lost his son to a car accident, a reporter on the scene asked him how he was doing he said, "I'm doing fine" and in his "next life" I hope my son will be better off." He was speaking of "reincarnation," meaning the rebirth of his son's soul in a new body.[17] This philosophical teaching says, "The nature of a person's next existence which could be [human or animal] through reincarnation is determined by their "karma," defined as the force generated by a person's actions in their present life. This is widely practiced in Hinduism and Buddhism.[18]From time to time you will hear the word "Karma" used in media commercials, or in jest and American slang.

Another religious philosophy causing much confusion in the American church is the New Age religion; an international social movement began in the 1970's.The merging of ideas from Asian religions and Western interpersonal psychology are often cited as its founders. Because its beliefs and customs are integrated or blended from other cultures, the New Age movement represents the beliefs and customs of many different cultures with the aim to form a multicultural global community [church].

Multiculturalism

Among the core values guiding this multicultural community is holism, a oneness of humans with nature, one universal set of religious beliefs, peace, harmony, and an orientation to the future.[19] Multi-cultures have always been the makeup of America, but Christianity and our biblical worldview were primarily based on the one an only God of the Christian faith. Today multi-cultures have evolved into multiculturalism with its many gods. This philosophy is working overtime in high places trying not only to displace the Christian faith but destroy it! Its many adherents in this country have made great strides over the years through media, academia, government and various anti-God and anti-Christ groups to silence the God of Abraham, Isaac, and Jacob in America.

Christianity is unique in the fact that it is not a religion in the traditional sense – but a *holy* life of *righteousness* in Christ Jesus. Religion consists of adherents who try to appease God by doing things to "reach up" and impress Him to gain favor through works-righteousness. Christianity's God came down to us! We come not in our own righteousness, but in Him and in His! We come by faith counting on Him, His righteousness, and His undeserved mercy and grace toward us.

If we claim ungodly self-righteousness as so many are doing, then we should check and see what God's Word has to say about it. I'm sure we've all heard Isaiah 64:6: *"All our righteousness is like filthy rags."* Filthy, dirty rags are hazardous to your health. They are not just dirty; they breed diseases, destruction and death.

Christ Himself wraps [those who believe in Him and accept Him as their Savior and Lord] in His righteousness (see 2 Corinthians 5:21). Other than His righteousness in us – there will never be anything other than filthy rags. If our thoughts are anything different, then we have deceived ourselves.

Spiritless Christianity

The challenge facing us as witnessing New Testament believer-priests is whether we will offer Jesus Christ [as the Redeemer who liberates us from sin and its power] or some spiritless substitute? Barna research shows that eighty-two percent of Americans believe Benjamin Franklin's aphorism, "God helps those who help themselves," is biblical. A growing number of Americans believe the lies that:

- All people pray to the same God, no matter what name they use for that spiritual being.
- If a person is generally good or does enough good for others during their lifetime, they will earn their place in heaven.

In his book, *Christless Christianity,* Michael Horton offers seven reasons for the diminishing American spirituality:

1. Most don't read and heed the Bible.
2. America is Christian in name only.
3. Our preference is spiritual experience over biblical knowledge.
4. We seek comfort overgrowth.
5. If faith doesn't come on our terms, then we reject it.
6. We have ruled ourselves the ultimate rulers of our own experiences.
7. We parallel the Pharisees of apostolic times.[20]

"A people that value its privileges above its principles soon lose both."
– President Dwight D. Eisenhower

You shall be My witnesses

In these days of increasing apostasy and false teaching, those who love God's truth will not be liked for speaking truth. But we can't let that stop us from doing the work of the kingdom that we are called and equipped by the Holy Spirit to do in His power:

- Witnessing His Word
- Sharing His love with others

Since Jesus's victory over Satan on Calvary, Satan knows that he cannot conquer the people of God, but he continues:

- To contaminate our testimonies.
- To discourage and uproot us.
- To make many of us retreat into our sacred four walls.

As we saw in the research in prior sections many pastors and local churches are disengaging from the cultural and societal conversations.

This is not the time for us to distance ourselves individually or corporately from a world that so desperately needs to see the light. Things I would have never thought possible twenty or thirty years ago are now the norm. This is true in much of the church as well as in the culture around us.

These things have so discouraged the hearts of many pastors and other church leaders that they give in making it very difficult for the local churches to keep moving forward. OH! But it's in times like these days of challenge that our training, preparation and experience as "living sacrifices" come in and blesses the kingdom of God. The Scripture says,

"Now thanks be to God who always leads us in triumph in Christ" (II Corinthians 2:14).

God will *always* lead His people into victory and triumph in Christ. As I warned several times in earlier sections the Church must be prepared at every level. We are to be fully engaged. Our eyes focused on the Christ-given task ahead ready to work in the harvest. We must put away all doubt and unbelief. Like the runner, we must pace ourselves and develop that second wind and complete the course! This was not always true in my life but thank the Lord that I was pulled from carnality and transformed into a seeker of the deeper things of God. Praise God, I am conditioned and love God and the truth even when it hurts and even when it is not popular. The rest of Second Corinthians 2:14 says,

"Through us [God] diffuses the fragrance of His knowledge in every place."

God leads us to victory so we might be His dispensers of His fragrance; this is God's intention for His people:

- That we dispense His fragrance [*revealed* truth] throughout this old sinful world.
- We must spend time with Him so that we can also carry His presence wherever we go also.
- Living the *revealed* truth, we teach, preach and talk about should make us standout, to the notice of all around us.

In other chapters of this book I have referenced Jude's writings, so it is fitting that we close this section with his admonition to his people.

He does not begin by denouncing; he seeks to win and save souls. The great objective of the gospel – as its ambassadors – is to call people to be reconciled to God.

He wanted the people to remember the words spoken before of the apostles of our Lord Jesus Christ. They prophesied of these mockers who would come in the last time, who would be refuted and condemned when they are shown to be at variance with the "most holy faith," a body of authoritative teachings by Christ and the apostles.

The mockers see no connection between spirituality and morality (v. 4). Jude begins by urging his people to remember. Don't be caught off guard by what is happening, be real! Jude, however, labels these mockers worldly people having no Spirit.

"These are they
who separate
themselves,
sensual,
having not the Spirit"(v.19).

Their overall satanic assignment recorded in Romans 1:25 is to, *change the truth of God into a lie and worship and serve the creature more than the Creator, who is blessed forever, Amen.*

Defend the Faith

Jude's counsel to his people echoes through the centuries to the Christian church everywhere today. His counsels individually and corporately are very simple, wise and doable:

- We are to build ourselves up in the most holy faith. Build on the foundation that has been laid, our Lord and Savior, Jesus Christ.
- We are to pray in the Holy Spirit. The Holy Spirit is our inward teacher. He enables our spirit to discern the deep things of God. He leads us into all truth. He brings us to proper dependence on God and communion with God without which the believer-priest has no foundation and no substance.
- We are to keep ourselves in the love of God. It requires our attention if God's love and power are to be effective in us.
- We are to humble ourselves before a Holy God for we deserve nothing.

- Our hope in the mercy of Christ Jesus is the final sustainer of any believer.
- We are to be compassionate toward those who have fallen to the heresy.
- We must consecrate ourselves as our Lord did. We are saved to serve. Like the apostle Paul we must "become all things to all men, that [we] might by all means save some" (see I Corinthians 9:22).
- We must defend the truth of God's Word.
- Be filled with the Spirit.

Our best defense [truth] is our best offense. So the final counsel again is not condemnation of the deceivers but redemption defending the faith through convincing arguments, showing mercy, and countering and exposing error – through living the clear, penetrating light of truth about the one and only true God, and Jesus Christ, our Lord and Savior. Emphasis added throughout.

The last promise and the last prayer of the Bible

God in Christ comprises everything that goes between the Alpha and the Omega, as well as being the First and the Last. This expresses God's fullness, comprehensiveness, and all-inclusiveness. He is the Source of all things to their appointed end. The Holy Spirit gives an invitation to all who will come by faith,

"And the Spirit and the bride say, "Come!"
And let him who hears say, "Come!"
And let him [or her] who thirsts come.
Whoever desires, let him [or her]
Take the water of life
freely."
– Revelation 22:17

The Benediction

Only God can keep us from falling. In spite of our insufficiency, finiteness, and sinfulness He can, and He will present us on that Day before the presence of His glory without blemish. The keeping and perfecting power of life is in the hands of a God who guards what is His own – and finishes what He has begun. Here is a benediction which not only affirms something about God; it also assures believer-priests of something about themselves.

The benediction is a "good word." That is the reason it is used at the end of a worship service as believer-priests part one from the other:

- They take with them the spirit of the church.
- They are to remember that God will never forsake them.
- They are to remember that He guards them and will present them before His presence without sin.
- True believer-priests live in the benediction of God.

In v. 24 we have the present anticipatory reality. The believer-priest's confidence is accurately voiced:

To him who is able to keep you from falling and to present you before his glorious presence without fault and with great joy – to the only God our Savior be glory, majesty, power and authority, through Jesus Christ our Lord, before all ages, now and forevermore! And to that all believer-priests who share the author's faith will respond with a resounding AMEN!

REFLECTION AND DISCUSSION QUESTIONS: CHAPTER 23

1. Discuss reincarnation's affect on Christianity in the nation's schools.

2. What affect has multiculturalism affected your church?

3. God Himself is the Source of those who are His.

4. Discuss the world's general reaction toward God's revealed truth.

5. Discuss how is Jude's reaction to the false teachers differs from most today.

6. I can apply this lesson to my life by:

7. Closing Statement of Commitment:

NOTES

INTRODUCTION

CHAPTER 2

[1] Major W. Ian Thomas, *The Saving Life of Christ* (Zondervan Publishing House 1988) 22

[2] W. E. Vine's Greek Grammar and Dictionary (Thomas Nelson Publishers 2012) 267
Note: Advocate *(paraklesis GK)* means "a calling to one's side." Either used as "an exhorter, or consolation, comfort." Page 267

[3] Vines Dictionary: Note: Intercession means "to make a petition" or "intercede on behalf of another." In Romans 8:27 of the Holy Spirit's intercessory work for the saints and Christ's similar intercessory work in Hebrews 7:25. Page 409

CHAPTER 4

[4] Watchman Nee, *The Normal Christian Life* (American Edition, Tyndale House Publishers, 1977) 13-15.

CHAPTER 5

[5] Henry T. Blackaby and Claude V. King, *Experiencing God* (Broadman and Holman Publishers 1998) 100

[6] Jay R. Leach, *Manifestation of the True Children of God* (Trafford Publishers 2015) 186

[7] Jay R. Leach, *How Should We Then Live* (iUniverse Publishers 2010) 45

CHAPTER 7

[8] Blackaby & King, *Experiencing God,* pages 142-143

CHAPTER 11

[9] W.E. Vine's Dictionary: Note: to make of a like form. (see Phil. 3:10) 276

[10] Jay R. Leach, *Narrow is the Way* (Trafford Publishers 2014) 42

[11] William J. Federer, *Change to Chains* (Amerisearch, St. Louis, MO. 2011) 150

CHAPTER 12

[12] Steve Sonderman, *Mobilizing Men for One-on-One Ministry* (Bthaney House Publishers 2010) 67

CHAPTER 15

[13] Earle E. Cairns, PH. D., *Christianity Through the Centuries* (Zondervan Publishing House 1973) 98

[14] Ibid 99

[15] Charles Haynes, Director of the Religious Freedom Center of the Newseum Institute. Accessed from the Fayetteville Observer.

CHAPTER 20

[16] W.E. Vine's Dictionary note: denotes a tradition of "apostolic teaching in 2 Thessalonians 2:15, of Christian doctrine. Page 585

[17] Webster's New Explorer Dictionary and Thesaurus (Merriam-Webster, Inc. 1999)page 442

[18] Ibid. page 287

[19] Religion a Cross Cultural Dictionary (Oxford University Press, New York 1998) page 145

CHAPTER 23

[20] Michael Horton, *Christless Christianity* (Baker Books 2008) page 31